Other books by Colleen J. McElroy

OVER THE LIP OF THE WORLD

OVER THE LIP OF THE WORLD

AMONG THE STORYTELLERS OF MADAGASCAR

COLLEEN J. MCELROY

A SAMUEL AND ALTHEA STROUM BOOK

University of Washington Press
Seattle and London

This book is published with the assistance of a grant from the Stroum Book Fund, established through the generosity of Samuel and Althea Stroum.

The color section was supported by a grant from the University of Washington's Institute of Ethnic Studies in the United States. The author also expresses her appreciation to the Fulbright Foundation and the Council for International Exchange of Scholars for their support of this project.

Library of Congress Cataloging-in-Publication Data
Over the lip of the world : among the storytellers of Madagascar / Colleen J. McElroy.
p.   cm.
Includes bibliographical references.
ISBN 0-295-97824-4 (alk. paper)
1. Oral tradition—Madagascar.   2. Storytelling—Madagascar.
3. Mythology, Malagasy.   I. McElroy, Colleen J.
GR357.09   1999
398.2'09691—dc21   99-14595
                                                   CIP

The paper used in this publication meets the minimum requirements of the American National Standard for Information Sciences—Permanence of Paper for Printed Library Materials, ANSI Z39.48-1984.

CONTENTS

ILLUSTRATIONS

ix

Black and white illustrations:

INTRODUCTION

MORNING RICE: MADAGASCAR
Husks swishing like a dancer's skirts
A lemur rustles the spiny grass
The murmur of red dust brushing sisal

In the spring of 1993, I undertook a Fulbright research project to Madagascar in order to explore Malagasy oral traditions and myths. During my visit, I recorded stories and song-poems from village folk artists as well as interviews with Malagasy ethnographers and poets. This book is a result of my travels to various parts of the country: from the capital, Antananarivo, across the high plateau country of central Madagascar to Nosy Bé and the northern isles, and to the coast at Fort Dauphin at the southernmost tip. However, the book is not, by any means, an attempt to define the people of Madagascar by political or social order, or to discern historical classifications and patterns in Malagasy verbal arts. Instead, it offers examples of the oral traditions currently practiced in several regions on the island; specifically, translations of poems and stories that depict heroism and morality, love and revenge, and the magic of tricksters and shapechangers, accompanied by photographs of those storytellers and poets who shared their art with me.

As the great-granddaughter of African descendants who survived diaspora on American soil, the similarity of appearance between myself and a population bound by Africa on one side, and by migrations of people crossing the vast Pacific and Indian Oceans on the other, worked in my favor. In fact, I was often mistaken for Malagasy (Bara or Sakalava). This sense of commonality gained me entry to villages and meeting places of folklorists and storytellers, and added a new dimension to my understanding of a country that Westerners think of as isolated, a country facing Africa across Mozambique Channel, the infamous route taken by pirates, slavers, and seafaring traders.

Then, as now, Madagascar was not easily reached, and legends about its location were tied to the mystique of those early sailors who landed on its shores, and spoke of it as "paradise." Historically, it has been called by various names: Lumuria, Gondwanaland, Tanindrazana. Today, the Red Island, as it was dubbed by NASA astronauts, is officially known as the Democratic Republic of Madagasikara, and the people are Malagasy. In the Southern Hemisphere about 240 miles off the coast of Africa, the island is the last land mass before Antarctica. It is the fourth largest island in the world, measuring 227,760 square miles, approximately the combined size of the western states of California, Oregon, and Washington. The land of the Malagasy stretches from Toamasina and Nosy Boraha on the eastern coast to Morondava in the West, and from Antsiranana (Diégo Suarez) and the island of Nosy Bé in the north to Toliara and Faux Cap at the southern tip. The terrain ranges from the humid, tropical coastline to the more arid plateau region in the central part of the island.

Historically, Madagascar has been on the trade routes from India and North Africa, and from Southeast Asia and the Pacific—a link evidenced by its people, and by cultural patterns commonly found in Malaysia and the Pacific, as well as Africa. The population of about nine million is a mixture of African, Malayo-Polynesian, Arab, and Indian descent. Some eighteen ethnic groups are linked together under a central government in Antananarivo, or Tana, the capital, where the population numbers more than 800,000. Tana is the political hub of the country, a bustling city of districts and suburbs, and it was from Tana that I began my research into Malagasy oral traditions.

While most foreign researchers continue to concentrate on the flora and fauna of Madagascar, some, particularly the French, examine the

Antsiranana
(Diégo Suarez)

Nosy Bé   Vohémar

● Ambanja

Antalaha

Analalava

Mahajanga (Majunga) ● ● Port-Bergé

L. Mangtsa   Mananara

Marovoay

Soalala   Nosy Boraha
                                      (Ste. Marie Is.)

Maevatanana   Fénérive

                    L. Alaotra

Maintirano   Ambatondrazaka
                    Toamasina
                    (Tamatave)

Ambohimanga
            Ivato   Brickaville
Antananarivo
Arivonimamo   Moramanga
                     Vatomandry

Tsiribihina R.
            Betafo ● ● Antsirabe

Morondava   *L. Tritriva*
                 Ambositra

                          Mananjary

            Fianarantsoa

Morombe   Manakara
        Ihosy   Vohipeno
Mangoky R.
                         Farafangana

Toliara (Tuléar)
                Betroka
Onilahy R. Sakoa

                    0   50 100   200
                    ┣━━┳━━┳━━━━━━━┫ KILOMETERS
                    0   50 100   200 MILES

Ampanihy ●
        ● Antanimora
            Taolañaro
            (Fort Dauphin)

CHANEL DE MOZAMBIQUE

INDIAN OCEAN

Betsiboka R.

Mananara R.

riddles and proverbs of the Malagasy. However, there are very few English-language researchers who focus on the verbal arts and cultural attributes of the people. Of course, I could not completely ignore the island's unique flora and fauna. I will never forget the morning I awoke to find five or six of Madagascar's hissing cockroaches, the size of half-dollars, clinging to my braided hair, or the one afternoon at the Berenty Reserve when I turned to find about a dozen ring-tailed lemurs on the road behind me, mimicking my pace by stopping when I stopped and moving faster when I pretended to hurry. But as fascinating as I found such creatures as bug-eyed chameleons glaring like E.T.s, or two-foot-long walking sticks hanging from trees like pale yellow vines, my interests were centered on the folklore that depicted the *angano* (stories), *arira* (fables), *tantara* (legends), poems and *hainteny*, including the song-poems of *hiragasy* as well as *kabary*, the poetic oratory of ceremonial traditions.

As I gathered material, I constantly changed my definition of what constituted a folktale. I came prepared to see how folktales were currently being presented within the various cultural regions of Madagascar. I was interested in the most living and mobile folktales, the feedback or oral traditions through generations, the borrowing and reinterpretation of foreign elements. Initially, I had planned to concentrate only on those folktales that employed trickster figures, shapechangers, and time travelers. Eventually, I expanded my research to include dance and song-poems, or performance pieces. Even so, my focus was much narrower than the full range of verbal arts traditionally presented by Madagascar's storytellers and musicians.

With the exception of three poets included here, I did not investigate the verbal arts of *ohabolana* and *hainteny*, the many poetic proverbs and riddles that express truth metaphorically. And only to a limited extent did I examine *kabary*, the ritual art of oratory, outside of the context of what was included in folktales. With the exception of Leonard Fox's

Hainteny: The Traditional Poetry of Madagascar (1990), Lee Haring's *Verbal Arts in Madagascar* (1992), and Lesley A. Sharp's *The Possessed and the Dispossessed: Spirits, Identity, and Power in a Madagascar Migrant Town* (1993), very little has been done by American researchers to explore forms of Malagasy oral traditions that are not connected to the realm of folk music. Recently, the international music scene has experienced a surge of interest in Malagasy music, particularly from such artists as Rossy, a musician who combines traditional Malagasy instrumentation and melodies with contemporary music and is popular in his native country as well as abroad. And just as the music of Madagascar has retained traditional forms, so has language provided the verbal instrumentation of traditional arts for current storytellers and poets, including dramatized versions of folktales, complete with heroes, damsels in distress, shapechangers, and villains.

One question invariably is postulated: Are these the real stories? No folklorist assumes that the original story has survived without variation. Just as Malagasy musicians have incorporated Western instruments, such as the electric guitar, into the repertoire of traditional music, storytellers utilize the changes in culture to embellish traditional folktales and poems. The Finnish folklorist Antti Aarne considered variants as ways in which the storyteller may: (1) omit details through sheer forgetfulness; (2) add details, whether invented or borrowed, often at the beginning or end of the story; (3) multiply details by a favorite number, such as three; (4) reverse the roles of two major characters; (5) change a character from animal to human or vice versa; (6) add culturally specific or modern details; or (7) be forced into further changes to keep the story consistent (cited from John Bierhorst, *The Mythology of South America*, 1988, p. 97). In some cases, these variants depend on audience availability. The more familiar the audience is with the story, the more likely they will be to participate in its telling, forcing the storyteller to alter the details accordingly. These changes occur with or without the presence of an outside researcher, for in no instance does the original story survive intact.

The mere fact of orality implies the presence of variants. What does survive, however, is the stem of the story and the tale type. The details may vary, but not enough to obscure the original outline.

The stories, or *angano*, included here can be divided roughly into two types: *tapasiry*, tales about the conduct of individuals and social ethics; and *tantara*, myths which explain the origins of things, animals, rituals, good and evil, particularly the relationship between people and magical or divine powers. Both types of stories were filled with the poetic allusions commonly reflected in the proverbs and riddles of the oral tradition. Frequently, various aspects of the *angano* were reconstructions of riddles, one of the characteristic patterns of Malagasy verbal arts found in *hainteny*, the traditional verbal art of poems and proverbs. In addition, some tales included trickster stories, tales about clever characters or characters who had limited physical powers and had to live by their wits. All of these legends followed the pattern of Malagasy oral tradition in which every being, alive or inanimate, has some degree of *hasina* (sacred power), thus giving the tale, or *angano*, its legendary magic. And finally, while the names of characters might have differed from one region to another, the folktales were similar in content.

Most of the stories are brief, their endings often abrupt, their motives sometimes more riddle than logic. Like any traditional folktale, these stories dispense with a preamble. The storyteller offers the tale and asks you to believe what you will. This request to suspend disbelief, along with several other conventions, is consistent with folktales from other countries. There were, in fact, several elements present in Malagasy folktales that can be found universally in stories of the oral tradition. They are often rife with metaphors and riddles and, like African American folktales, contain a rhetoric of indirection and double meaning (Callahan 1988). The numbers two and three are commonly used in storytelling, as in twins, or three wishes and three sons. Another example is the use of natural objects, such as trees, which assume strange forms and take on the cloak of magic. Actions are emphasized and prolonged by repetition, as in

Jack and the Beanstalk when the beanstalk grows "so tall, so tall," or in the Brer Rabbit tale when the rabbit flees into the woods "lickety split, lickety split, lickety split." As with tales from other countries, the least powerful character in a Malagasy tale can become most powerful, offering a lesson in morality and bravery that renders the character stronger than the strongest. In terms of natural elements, the sky is not the only source of mythic origins. Spirits also exist beneath the earth's surface, especially in the underwater realm. The beautiful woman who materializes out of the water can exist in the same cultural setting that allows monsters to emerge from whirlpools, or peasants to be swept into the water at a spirit's caprice. These stories both entertain and teach. They are legends through which children can learn the importance of social roles, and tales which reinforce the adult's sense of responsibility to social and moral commitment, particularly regarding family and ancestors.

In a blend of fantasy and reality, the *angano* of Madagascar can be connected to the history of a particular region, and to the country's respect for social customs that both strengthen authority and allow ordinary people to protest against established order. But most important, there were some common threads in the *angano*—whether told by village storytellers, orators, choral singers, or university scholars. Each spoke of morality and recognized the influence of ancestors on every aspect of life. *Ny maty sy ny velona*, a Malagasy phrase which translates as "the dead and the living," demonstrates how the ancestors, the dead, assume the position of importance, in contrast with the Westernized notion of "the living and the dead," which places the living first and the dead as an afterthought. The verbal arts of Madagascar reinforce the cultural link to ancestral spirits, the *razana*. This link is clear throughout the verbal arts: in the oratory of *kabary*, the ritual of *famadihana* (loosely translated as "turning of the bones"), the song-poems of *hiragasy*, and the *fitenin-drazana*, or sayings of the ancestors. For the Malagasy, this connection between ancestors and the living provides scriptures from the past that teach the people what they need to know about the present, and leads them safely into the future. And so, as the Malagasy say, "A folktale is like the chameleon—it unfolds with one eye on the past and the other eye on the future."

In most instances, I have presented these stories and memoirs (my field-notes) by region, recalling my journey through various parts of the country. The photographs that accompany this material are offered as a way of strengthening the landscape of the Malagasy legends, and a way of showing my appreciation to those storytellers and poets who so kindly allowed me to walk with them for a brief time. I have followed the cautions of Emerson, Fretz, and Shaw as stated in their book, *Writing Ethnographic Fieldnotes* (1995): "In writing fieldnotes, ethnographers have as their primary goal, description rather than analysis . . . not simply from good memory but more crucially from learning to remember dialogue and movement like an actor, to see colors and shapes like a painter, and to sense moods and rhythms like an poet."

This material is but a glimpse into the richness and texture of a country where the oral tradition of storytelling is a direct link to the ancestral aesthetics of the culture as well as to everyday life, the land, and its people. They are stories that have lingered for centuries, tied to the geography from which they have risen, fixed in place if not in time. For this reason, each story is preceded by a memoir, an accounting of my travels, set within the context of the region and the events that led me to the storyteller. These fieldnotes are not intended as explanations of the stories, but as memoirs, narratives that bring the reader closer to the cultural context of the stories and poems. Finally, all of the material is a way of bringing Madagascar into perspective from its distant location, a way to offer an additional connection between the teller of the tale and English-language readers' intellectual involvement with Malagasy oral tradition.

I am indebted to M. Haingolalao Rasolonirinarimanana, M. Serge, and M. Simon Ramarijaona for their assistance in mapping my travels across the island of Madagascar. I also would like to express my gratitude for the assistance of M. Roland Razafintsalama of the African-American Institute, U.S.I.S. Antananarivo, and Mme. Arianne Rafalimanana as well as Teddy, Rafily, Maria, Bernadette, and Mira of the Le Karthala Pension staff, who provided me with a home away from home. And a very special note of appreciation to Stephen Rush of Crossroads Travel for his years of patience and assistance in routing my journeys, both near and distant. I also offer thanks to Beverly Mendheim for her helpful suggestions, and to Stephen Rowland for providing additional photographs during the last two weeks of my visit to Madagascar. Additional thanks go to Hayley Mitchell and Mira Shimabukuro, who were not daunted by reading handwritten notes that seemed to have been scribbled underwater; to Janie Smith and Laura McKee for being, as always, editors extraordinaire; and to Mary Baylor for her invaluable assistance with cataloguing and indexing the material.

Above all, none of this research would have been completed without the wonderful assistance of my translator and companion, Mlle. Tiana Flora Tsizaza. Without her help in mapping with me the bridges and borders of language, and the many roads of Madagascar, this project might have floundered in the Mozambique Channel halfway to Nosy Bé. Mlle. Tsizaza, vous êtes un bijou.

In the course of my research, I learned to follow the Malagasy caution of Sennen Andriamirado: "Enjoy hospitality in the full, but know how to remain a dignified outsider." This outsider discovered many beautiful moments when language transcended cultural differences, when folktales were truly the steed that carried me to a far country.

Colleen J. McElroy
Seattle, Washington

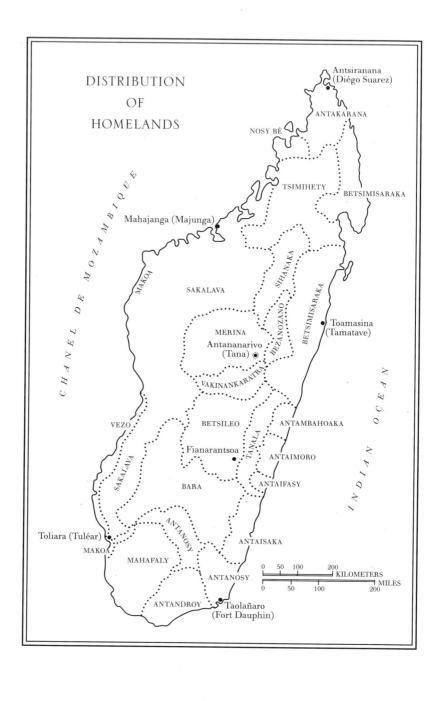

DISTRIBUTION
OF
HOMELANDS

Antsiranana
(Diégo Suarez)

ANTAKARANA

NOSY BÉ

TSIMIHETY

BETSIMISARAKA

CHANEL DE MOZAMBIQUE

Mahajanga (Majunga)

MAKOA

SAKALAVA

SIHANAKA

BEZANOZANO

BETSIMISARAKA

MERINA
Antananarivo
(Tana)

Toamasina
(Tamatave)

VAKINANKARATRA

INDIAN OCEAN

VEZO

BETSILEO

ANTAMBAHOAKA

TANALA

Fianarantsoa

ANTAIMORO

SAKALAVA

BARA

ANTAIFASY

ANTANOSY

Toliara (Tuléar)

MAKOA

MAHAFALY

ANTAISAKA

0   50   100   200
KILOMETERS
0   50   100   MILES
200

ANTANOSY

ANTANDROY

Taolañaro
(Fort Dauphin)

THE TAPESTRY OF
LANGUAGES IN TRANSLATION

A traveler is heading for the market in Antananarivo, the capital city of Madagascar. At the outskirts of the city, his footprints are shadowed in red dust. As he comes closer to town, the dusty road changes to cobblestones. It is dawn. The city is just beginning to awaken. A rooster crows. A dog sniffs at the traveler's heels. He sees another man walking toward him, a figure still shadowy in the early morning light. The traveler shouts hello, speaking in the manner of those who live in the Highlands. "*Manahoana Tompoko*," he says to the man approaching him. The man does not answer. Again the traveler says hello. "*Manakôry*," he calls, hailing the stranger this time in the dialect of the Mahajanga region. The man comes closer, but still does not answer. So the traveler tries his greeting in two other dialects: "*Akory lahaly*," he says. "*Mbôla tsara*." Now they are as close as a handshake, but still the stranger does not answer. Yet the traveler persists: "Hello. Hello," he calls again. ("*Akory anareo. Salama va!*") Will I be ignored? the traveler thinks as the man passes, his head held high. Well, if he believes he is a king, the traveler thinks, I will address him as we used to address one who was king. "*Tsarava Tompoko*," he says and mockingly tips his hat as if he has indeed encountered the king. But to his surprise, only then does the passerby smile, for the traveler has greeted him as royalty.

This little tale of language and circumstance is an illustration of the linguistic diversity found in Madagascar, where a spectrum of dialects are united by a common geography under one language umbrella: Malagasy. In most English-language books on Madagascar, language is an afterthought, rarely if ever described as a significant element in understanding Malagasy culture and history. This book, however, takes into consideration the complexities and differences of Malagasy and English. Indeed, discussing some of the considerations of translating from Malagasy to English may assist readers in understanding the nuances of language used in these stories and poems. Certainly, a brief introduction to the Malagasy language may illustrate the importance of the oral tradition, and more specifically the importance of the orator or storyteller in a country where the oral tradition has been maintained.

Lee Haring, among others, describes Malagasy language as containing eighteen dialects, but allowing for the more recent investigations by such groups as the researchers at the Musée d'Art et d'Archeologie in Antananarivo, there may be, by all counts, as many subdialects under those major dialects. In some cases, the differences between dialects are subtle; in others, the distances are as vast as the thousand mile length of the island and the many ethnic groups residing there. The folktales and poems contained in this book are taken from those Malagasy dialects spoken primarily in the region of the Highlands, the southern and southeastern regions, and the northwestern coastal areas of the country — specifically Betsileo, Antaimoro, Sakalava (Antakarana), Merina, Vakinankaratra, Mahafaly, Tsimihety, and Vezo. Understanding dialect difference between regions was an essential ingredient in translating these folktales, because quite often the stories were empowered by those differences. For that reason, the discussion that follows is restricted to a brief examination of some of the differences between dialects in terms of the complexity of recording, transcribing, and translating material from the oral to written forms.

Linguists agree that there is no task more complicated than translation. Burton Raffel, in *The Art of Translating Poetry* (1988), goes so far as to say, "If every human language is distinct (as it is) in structure, sound, and vocabulary, and if every language contains unique features, then clearly, it is literally impossible to fully render anything written in one language to another." But despite these obstacles, translation allows us to cross corridors of culture with a better sense of where we are going and where we will be when we arrive. It is a task worth the undertaking, for as Thomas Mann said, "Who would wish to discourage the peoples of the world from translating, merely because it is fundamentally impossible?"

The Malagasy language is rich with proverbs and poetic images, some taken from the sayings of the old ones, the ancestors, but all stemming from a love of the oratory. For a folklorist, understanding language differences both enriches and complicates the study of the oral tradition. Most of the material in this book was transcribed from the spoken word, a factor further complicating the task of translating the material into written form. And in the case of Malagasy-English translation, that task is made more difficult by the need to shift from the Malayo-Polynesian language family, which includes Malagasy, to the Indo-European language family, which includes English. Furthermore, there has been little formal study to date of the linguistic attributes of some Malagasy dialects; and the available, but limited, Malagasy-English dictionaries, which are based primarily on the Merina dialect of the Highland region, do not incorporate the linguistic differences intrinsic to other dialects of Malagasy. From time to time, recognizing the ethnographic diversity of the island, both British and French scholars have questioned the supposed linguistic unity of Madagascar (Haring, *Verbal Arts in Madagascar*). But while the dialects of Madagascar can be as varied as the ethnography of the island, those dialects share a number of characteristics, such as markers of time, gender, plurality, and the inclusion of ancestors in present as well as past tense. On the other hand, these dialects do not always share the same characteristics of sounds, phrasing, and associations. Thus translators must have an "ear" for the spoken language—a practical knowledge of the oral aspects of the language.

Phonology: Some Elements of Sounds in Malagasy

Madagascar is a country still famous for its verbal arts, particularly folktales, proverbs, and poetry—traditions practiced throughout the island by orators respected for the energy and fluency of their art forms. Differences in how words are spoken, the sounds of the language, are especially important when working in those Malagasy dialects that are regional, and primarily restricted to the oral tradition. Translators must take into account that while the subject of the story, poem, or proverb may remain the same in different regions of the country, the words used to describe the subject may differ.

One factor that separates dialects is the distinctive feature called radical consonants, sounds that shift between dialects. These shifts may be dictated by regional differences as well as differences in meaning.

Recognizing word endings as a meaningful element is an important consideration for translators. Malagasy words end only with *y*, *o*, *a*, or *e*. In some instances, these sounds form the suffixes *ka*, *tra*, and *na*, which are known as light terminals. (See James Richardson, *A New Malagasy–English Dictionary*, 1885.) These suffixes are often mute, or silenced by sounds that precede or follow them. Both passive verbs and possessive pronouns are formed by specific word endings that may also be compressed or muted by the sounds that precede or follow them. Additionally, some prefix and suffix combinations may involve shifts in sound patterns between dialects. In Merina, for example, the word for "knee" is *lohalika*, using the suffix *ka*, but in Betsileo, it is *lohaleke*, with *ke* as a suffix. Likewise, in Merina, the suffix *tra*, as in *peratra* ("finger ring"), becomes *peratsa* in Mahafaly, with the suffix *tsa*. Another example is the Merina word *tandindona* ("a person's shadow"), which in Mahafaly holds a neutral (muted) suffix to become *tandilo*. Understanding word endings is particularly important in the translation of poems that follow specific rhyme forms. In Malagasy the key to the rhyme scheme depends primarily on the suffix pattern, as opposed to English, where the rhyme depends primarily on the vowel pattern, usually of the root word. And so, while Malagasy poetry may employ the traditional rhyme schemes of English poetry, translators must take into account the differences of stress and suffix patterns, the elision and liaison of Malagasy word structures as opposed to the staccato and legato rhythms of English (Raffel, *Art of Translating Poetry*). The translator strives to retain the music of the poetic language without distorting the contextual beauty of the poem.

According to Richardson, the missionary who compiled the Malagasy–English dictionary in 1885, "Malagasy does not allow the free combination of consonants commonly found in European languages . . . [and] the allowable combination of consonants are very few." By the same token, regional differences may be straightforward, consistent shifts in sounds. For example, *n* in Merina can become *ng*, *n*, or *ñ* in other dialects. These differences for Malagasy are similar to shifts in sound patterns between British English, American English, and Australian English for words that involve changes in sounds but not in meanings.

In addition to shifts in sound patterns or spelling, changes in how words are spoken also can involve changes in meaning between dialects. The word for "wife" or "husband," which is *vady* in Merina or Betsileo, becomes *valy* in Mahafaly. But in Sakalava, *valy* means "brother-in-law." A similar change is shown for the word *fintana*, which means "fish-hook" in Merina, while in the Vezo dialect the word for "fishhook" is *vintana*. But in a reverse shift, *vintana* in Merina, means "fate" or "destiny," an important word for anyone about the business of translating folktales and poetry. These are examples of the nuances of sound differences between Malagasy dialects. There are many shifts that involve only sound, but those which include word origins and meaning are more numerous. Where the shifts were dialect specific, present only in one dialect, and comparable sound patterns could not be found in the available dictionaries, translation depended on deriving the root word from the context of the phrase, and working from the standpoint of word patterns rather than sound patterns.

Morphology: Patterns of Words in Malagasy

Malagasy is invested with the same complexities of how words are formed as in Indo-European languages. In translating, however, it is necessary to put aside assumptions of certain word pattern categorizations based on Indo-European structures (Haring, *Verbal Arts in Madagascar*). For example, certain word patterns, such as the Indo-European auxiliary verbs "to be" and the "-ing" gerund forms, do not appear in Malagasy. In fact, for the non-native speaker of Malagasy dialects, it is often difficult when listening to spoken language to isolate verb forms—in the familiar sense of isolating verbs in Indo-European languages. For that reason, the translator exploring the oral tradition must have both a critical knowledge of the language and a practical knowledge of its elements.

Often, those forms are buried in a word by inclusion of syllables as prefix, suffix, or embedded syllables or morphemes. For certain verbs, embedded morphemes indicate that the subject is being voluntarily acted upon—as when the morpheme *in* is embedded in *babe* ("to go piggy back") becoming *binabe* ("to be carried piggy back"), and *om* embedded in *mitoera* ("to be quiet") becoming *mitomera* ("obliged to be quiet"). In both cases, the presence of the embedded morpheme changes the relationship of the action to the person involved in the action. In other words, the tone of the root word changes.

Certain word patterns are consistent between Malagasy dialects. For example, verb conjugation remains the same throughout most of the dialects. Prefixes are used to indicate past, present, and future time markers, as well as the indicative, nominative, and imperative moods, all of which are delineated within the three major divisions of active, passive, and relative voice. At the same time, however, verb conjugation creates serious ambiguities, which further complicates translation (see Richardson). In Malagasy, a single root verb may change in voice, mood, and case with changes in the speaker and the setting. Additionally, relative voice does not have a correspondence in Indo-European languages, but in Malagasy this form allows the speaker to be very concise. This complexity of verb conjugation represents one of the most difficult aspects of transcribing material to be translated from the oral tradition.

Another consistent element among dialects of Malagasy is the use of markers for plurality and gender. In Malagasy dialects, gender is not marked. Pronouns, such as *izy* and *aho*, can be "he, she, or it," with the distinction determined by context. By the same token, plurality markers do not employ the suffix "-s," as found in Indo-European languages. Instead, plurality is formed by context.

For Malagasy, the root word not only represents the smallest individually meaningful element of a word, but may also be used to set mood and voice within the context of a phrase. In some instances, repetition of the root word can change the mood of the phrase. For example, with repetition, the root word *mihazaka* ("to run") becomes *mihazakazaka*, implying the singular intent to run or to move speedily. Another example is the word *masina*, "farewell," which when repeated becomes *masimasina*, "goodbye goodbye." Repetition for emphasis is a common element in the oral tradition of many languages. In nursery rhymes, the hero may move "far away far away" to emphasize distance, while to set the stage as a "long long time ago" implies the distant past. In Malagasy, this type of emphasis can occur both as repetition of the root word, as in *mihazakazaka*, or repetition of an individual word, as in *taloha elaela be* ("long long time"), where the two words function as a single word. There are also words which, in certain circumstances, do not hold meaning but are considered morphological units because they function to alter the syntax of the utterance.

Syntax: Word Order in Sentences and Phrases

Convergence between meaning and the way words are arranged occurs most often with words that influence mood and the position of the speaker. To say that someone is possessed of a quality to a high degree, or to say someone does something in the best possible way, the word may be repeated and *dia* placed between the two words to emphasize the action. For example, "amazement," *gaga* becomes *gaga dia gaga*, "very amazed" or "astonished" when *gaga* is repeated with *dia* as the linking word. In some cases, *dia* when preceded by *ka* serves as a conjunction—"and," "and so," "then"—but in other instances, *dia* is used as a syntactical marker to change mood or emphasis. In another context, *dia* assumes a different grammatical function; in some cases serving as a relational word, putting elements of the sentence in perspective, and in other cases serving as an inversion marker.

Malagasy sentences are usually arranged as verb—object—subject, but when emphasis should be placed on something other than the verb, word order is inverted and the inversion indicated by adding *dia* or *no* after the subject. Both *dia* and *no* may become abstract particles and indicate an inversion of word order, rather than carry a specific meaning. The sentence *Manasa lamba ny vehivavy*, meaning "The women wash the clothes," follows the pattern of verb—object—subject. Inversion to subject—verb—object changes the sentence to *Ny vehivavy dia mansa lamba*, and *Ny vehivavy no manasa lamba* ("The clothes are washed by the women"). In the inversion that includes *dia*, the emphasis is on *what* they are doing (washing the clothes), while in the *no* inversion the emphasis is on *who* is performing the act in this case, the women. Word order inversion may differ between dialects. The Antaimoro and Antaisaka dialects use *da* instead of *dia*, and *no* rarely occurs in the Vezo dialect.

Semantics: Some Elements of Meaning and Metaphor in Malagasy

The most complicated element of any language, and the most important element in translation, is meaning, or semantics. In all languages, the denotative and connotative elements play upon the meaning of a given word: in isolation, within a phrase, in a specific situation, or used by different speakers. References of cultural, regional, and personal experiences are incorporated into the connotative or associative elements of semantics. Meanings change as experiences change. Moreover, dialects within the same language do not necessarily share the same meanings for a given word. This is true as well for dialects in Malagasy. The word *orana* means "rain" in Merina, but there is no literal equivalent in Sakalava, where the word *mahaleña* holds a more connotative association: "what makes one wet." Another example is the word *tsinjaka*, or "dance," in Sakalava; in Merina, the connotation changes the meaning of *tsinjaka* to "a dance of witches or frenzy." For the Merina, any other dance is called *dihy*. Some words remain the same, but there is a shift in meaning between one dialect and another. One such word is *jery*, which means "thought," except in Merina and Betsileo, where *jery* means "the way you look at something" or "your expression as you look at something."

Metaphorical context is particularly important when translating Malagasy into English. In the oral tradition of Madagascar, metaphors rule, and language is subject more to its connotative elements (associations) than to the denotative aspect (literal meaning). Language, indeed, becomes a means of simultaneously hiding and revealing thought so as to convey delicate and dangerous matters. (See Haring, *Verbal Arts in Madagascar*.) The verbal arts are built on eloquence, tact, and quick wit. For translators who are not grounded in the warp and weft of verbal arts, this has presented the most persistent barrier to understanding Malagasy; their confusion over metaphorical content often obscures the meaning of a given word. Many translators go no further than their initial encounter with a word, deriving meaning from the literal context. In three dictionaries, the word *sondriana* is defined as "to be in a brown study," "sitting in a brown study," or "absorbed in a brown study." *Diksionera Malagasy–English*, a limited edition published in 1992 in Madagascar, offers a secondary source for the word under *mahasondriana*, "to cause one to be absorbed or distracted." Since *maha* is a common verbal prefix, meaning "the ability or power to perform any action," *sondriana* is the root word meaning "absorbed or distracted." What, then, was the source of "a brown study"? Or better yet, what is a brown study? The most logical conclusion is that Richardson, in developing the 1885 version of the Malagasy–English dictionary, used the English reference for "brown study," roughly meaning "in a snit" or "sulking" or, as in the case of John Crowe Ransom's poem "Bells for John Whiteside's Daughter," even suggesting death itself (to be in a coffin). Richardson's loose interpretation of *sondriana* perhaps should be taken to mean "being inside or studying oneself." But whatever the reasons for the original misunderstanding, the metaphorical references were not based on the less negative connotative aspect of the Malagasy definition—to contemplate rather than to sulk—either by subject or situation. This is an example of what happens when translations are filtered through another language, and the original connotative and metaphorical significances are lost.

Metaphors can be a key element in translating folktales and poems. A metaphorical context increases the complications of translation, since metaphors are bound to the context, culture, history, and speaker's experiences. Often the metaphorical context will not hold true in translation. For example, the colors blue and white have different metaphorical associations in Malagasy than they do in English. In English, white may be attributed to purity or, at worst, small crimes, such as "a little white lie." While this association does not hold true for all speakers of English (see Ossie Davis, "The Language of Racism: The English Language Is My Enemy"), it is the accepted connotative implication. In Malagasy, white, or *fatsy*, may imply more negative connotations: *fotsy fanahy* ("two faced or hypocrite"), and *fotsy hotsatra* ("the walking dead"). In English, to be sad is to "sing the blues," while in Malagasy, the word *manga* ("blue") is used to say "You have a beautiful voice" (*Manga feo ianao*). Semantic elements, like those of phonology and morphology, are subject to the same contextual complexities—made even more complicated by the presence of the metaphorical elements of poetry, proverbs, and folktales.

Literal or denotative translations may provide a framework for the story or poem, but the metaphorical associations provide the texture and nuance of the work.

Even without these factors to consider, the shift from verbal to written language places other demands on folkloric translations. Malagasy, a tonal language, is graced with intonations and inflections, and translations must be framed by the idea that written language cannot capture all of the nuances of spoken language. Yet the translator must pay attention to these aspects of the storyteller's technique, keeping the circumstances of both the story and the telling of the story in mind. For example: stories that give advice may take one form when their listeners are adults and another when the audience is made up primarily of children. *Kabary*, formal dialogue and storytelling directed at adult audiences, is practiced throughout the country. The time that the story was presented—during the day or at the end of the day—may also be important to the context. The stories for women as they go about their work will differ from those for men at the end of the workday. Formal stories reserved for rituals such as weddings, for example, may determine the choice of language, and the metaphorical context. When transcribing recorded material, the translator must acknowledge these differences, keeping the colloquial language intact as much as possible, and yet also be aware of the more dramatic shifts that do influence interpretation. Without considering all of these differences, the stories included in this collection could not have been translated.

These stories are ones in which the ordinary was made extraordinary, the unbelievable made believable, the cycle of life and death shown as a cycle of the living in harmony with their ancestors. Each storyteller brought to these stories a little air of coolness and old tenderness, like the endless flow of waters that leave the rivers and flood the rice fields. The translator must not repay the storyteller's efforts by hindering the passage from storyteller to listener.

PROVERB: *Mitspa-doha-kaja-nitána.* You do not push back from the front of the boat that you have helped cross the river.

Colleen J. McElroy
Tiana Flora Tsizaza
Seattle, Washington

Selected Bibliography

Andriamirado, Sennen. *Madagascar Today*. Paris: Hippocrene Books, 1979.

Attenborough, David. *Bridge to the Past: Animals and People of Madagascar*. New York: Harper, 1962.

Bierhorst, John. *The Mythology of South America*. New York: William Morrow and Company, 1988.

Bradt, Hilary. *Guide to Madagascar*. London: Bradt Publications, 1997.

Callahan, John F. "The Spoken in the Written Wrod: African-American Tales and the Middle Passage from Uncle Remus: His Songs and Sayings to Conjure Women." In *In the African-American Grain: The Pursuit of Voice in Twentieth-Century Black Fiction,* pp. 25–61. Springfield: University of Illinois Press, 1988.

Davis, Ossie. "The Language of Racism: The English Language Is My Enemy." In *Language in America*, edited by Neil Postman, Charles Weingartner, and Terence P. Moran, p. 67. New York: Pegasus, 1969.

Doke, Clement M. "Lamba Folklore." *American Folklore Society Memoirs* 20 (1969).

Drury, Robert. *Madagascar: or, Robert Drury's Journal during Fifteen Years' Captivity on that Island.* London: T. F. Unwin; New York: Macmillan, 1890.

Dundes, Alan. *The Study of Folklore*. Englewood Cliffs, N.J.: Prentice-Hall, 1965.

Emerson, Robert M., Rachel I. Fretz, and Linda L. Shaw. *Writing Ethnographic Fieldnotes*. Chicago: University of Chicago Press, 1995.

English–Malagasy Phrase Book. Antananarivo: Madagascar Print and Press Company, 1973.

Faublée, J. *L'Ethnographie de Madagascar*. Paris: Bibliothèque D'outre-Mer, 1946.

Finn, Julio. "Jean-Joseph Rabearivelo: A Black Poet Under the Colonialist Yoke." In *Voices of Negritude*, edited by Julio Finn, pp. 1–7. London: Quartet, 1987.

Finnegan, Ruth. *Oral Poetry: Its Nature, Significance and Social Context*. Bloomington and Indianapolis: Indiana University Press, 1992.

Fox, Leonard. *Hainteny: The Traditional Poetry of Madagascar*. Lewisburg, Pa.: Bucknell University Press; London: Associated University Presses, 1990.

Haring, Lee. *Verbal Arts in Madagascar: Performance in Historial Perspective.* Philadelphia: University of Pennsylvania Press, 1992.

Huntington, Richard. *Gender and Social Structure in Madagascar.* Bloomington: Indiana University Press, 1988.

Hyde, Lewis. *Trickster Makes This World: Mischief, Myth, and Art.* New York: Farrar, Straus and Giroux, 1998.

Jolly, Alison. *A World Like Our Own.* New Haven: Yale University Press, 1980.

———. "Madagascar: A World Apart." *National Geographic.* February 1987, pp. 149–83 .

Kennedy, Ellen C. *The Negritude Poets.* New York: Thunder's Mouth Press, 1989.

Kent, Raymond K. *Early Kingdoms in Madagascar, 1500–1700.* New York: Holt, Rinehart and Winston, 1970.

———. *From Madagascar to the Malagasy Republic.* New York: Praeger, 1962.

Kesteloot, Lilyan. *Black Writers in French: A Literary History of Negritude.* Washington, D.C.: Howard University Press, 1991.

Krappe, Alexander H. *The Science of Folklore.* New York: W. W. Norton, 1964

Lanting, Frans. *Madagascar: A World Out of Time.* New York: Aperture Foundation, 1990.

Mack, John. "Ways of the Ancestors." *Natural History* 98, no. 4 (April 1989): pp. 24–31.

Marden, Luis. "Madagascar: Island at the End of the Earth." *National Geographic.* October 1967, pp. 443–87.

Mahdi, Waruno. *Morphophonologische Besonderheiten und historische Phonologie des Malagasy.* Berlin: D. Reimer, 1988.

McLeod, Lyons. *Madagascar and Its People.* New York: Negro Universities Press, 1969 [London, 1865].

Murphy, Dervla. *Muddling Through in Madagascar.* Woodstock: Overlook Press, 1989.

Mutibwa, Phares Mukasa. *The Malagasy and the Europeans: Madagascar's Foreign Relations, 1861–1895.* London: Longman, 1974.

Okpewho, Isidore. *African Oral Literature: Backgrounds, Character, and Continuity.* Bloomington and Indianapolis: Indiana University Press, 1992.

Paginton, K. *English–Malagasy Vocabulary.* Antananarivo: Trano Printy Loterana, 1970.

Radin, Paul, and James Johnson Sweeney. *African Folktales and Sculpture.* Princeton: Princeton University Press, 1954.

Raffel, Burton. *The Art of Translating Poetry.* University Park: Pennsylvania State University Press, 1988.

Rajaonah, Voahangy. "The Sacred Trees of Madagascar." *UNESCO Courier* May 1990, pp. 42–44.

Richardson, James, ed. *A New Malagasy–English Dictionary*. London: The London Missionary Society/Gregg Press Limited, 1885, reprint 1967.

Ryden, Kent C. *Mapping the Invisible Landscape: Folklore, Writing, and the Sense of Place*. Iowa City: University of Iowa Press, 1993.

Scheub, Harold. *African Oral Narratives, Proverbs, Riddles, Poetry and Song: An Annotated Bibliography*. New York: Macmillan, 1977.

Shapiro, Norman R. *Negritude: Black Poetry from Africa and the Caribbean*. New York: October House, 1970.

Sharp, Lesley A. *The Possessed and the Dispossessed: Spirits, Identity, and Power in a Madagascar Migrant Town*. Berkeley: University of California Press, 1993.

Shaw, George A. *Madagascar and France: With Some Account of the Island, Its People, Its Resources, and Development*. New York: Negro Universities Press, 1969.

Sheppherd, Joseph. *A Leaf of Honey and the Proverbs of the Rainforest*. London: Bahá'i Publishing Trust, 1988.

Stratton, Arthur. *The Great Red Island*. New York: Scribner, 1964.

Thompson, Virginia McLean, and Richard Adloff, *The Malagasy Republic: Madagascar Today*. Stanford: Stanford University Press, 1965.

Toelken, Barre. *The Dynamics of Folklore*. Boston: Houghton Mifflin Company, 1979.

Vaisse, Christian. *Madagascar*. Paris: Les Editions du Pacifique, 1990.

Vaovao, Andro. *An Elementary English–Malagasy Dictionary*. Antananarivo: Trano Printy Loterana, 1969.

———. *Diksionera Malagasy–English*. Antananarivo: Trano Printy Loterana, 1973.

Venuti, Lawrence, *The Translator's Invisibility: A History of Translation*. London and New York: Routledge Press, 1995.

Wake, Clive. *An Anthology of African and Malagasy Poetry in French*. London: Oxford University Press, 1965.

OVER THE LIP OF THE WORLD

CHAPTER I

AND ALL THE TOWNS BETWEEN

I arrived in Antananarivo, or Tana as the capital of Madagascar is called, in March 1993 at the end of the rainy season, an unhappy coincidence for someone like me coming from the rain forests of the Pacific Northwest. In the States, I knew how to clock the seasons by rain, knew the difference between a solid blanket of clouds that would not lift for days on end, and an uneven bank that signaled a sudden thunderstorm. But the sky above the Highlands of Madagascar was not the endless gray that shaped Northwest winters. The Southern Hemisphere lay under the sweep of summer rains, and the sky was a palette of changing colors and shapes, one moment as placid as a watercolor landscape, the next filled with thick, viscous clouds streaked with red and yellow spears of light like a Van Gogh painting. From the balcony of the La Karthala Pension, I watched the weather come in from the south and scatter across the hills, shadows of approaching rain smearing the whitewashed houses into a monochrome gray. And then the rain, sudden and fierce, streaking over the cup of the valley, threatening to turn everything into silt. But sometimes, as quickly as the rain shower began, it would end, and the sun would return to the Highlands as if the storm had never really happened—as if, indeed, the ancestors were smiling upon Antananarivo.

I came to expect those sudden bursts of rain, an almost welcome relief from the gritty air that usually cloaked the city. But the relief was always momentary; within the hour, the soil had soaked up the moisture, leaving Tana coated with a layer of pale ocher dust, punctuated by bright patches of green where a profusion of flowering cacti, poinsettia trees, and palms grew on the many balconies and parks terraced on the hillsides above the center of the city. Only in the low-lying areas—the swampy flats near the loading docks of the market, the freight yards spiderwebbed behind the train station, the windowless mud brick houses that skirted the city—was there evidence of the rain storm. In those places, the water was slow to run off, resisting the porous earth that beckoned it. In those places, the clay red soil was blackened by deposits of coal and firewood, and children who ran errands in the market ran barefoot through the muck, ignoring for a moment the work they had been sent to do. From my vantage point on the balcony, if I listened closely, I could hear their voices rising above the rush of traffic, the call of vendors, and the soldiers, stationed in the barracks between the pension and the market, answering the orders of the day.

Antananarivo—the city of a thousand warriors, the city of a thousand villages—was a city of red-tiled roofs and terraced hills circumscribed by circular roads separating the king's palaces and older houses of Upper Town from the government buildings, hotels, and the Zoma market of Lower Town. La Karthala Pension was located on the slope above the Zoma, not quite Upper Town but high enough to leave me with a view of the elementary school and army barracks on the side street above the market, high enough to allow me to see the sweep of land on the other side of Lower Town, picture perfect hillside houses crowded together in a seemingly chaotic sprawl that kept to its own sense of order. The main thoroughfares and arterial streets were crisscrossed by a spiderweb of hillside climbs, some no more than stone steps passable only by foot. But all the traffic spilled down to the Zoma. Everything, from roads and sidewalks to narrow stairways, radiated from the hub of the market. Under a canopy of white canvas umbrellas and peaked vendors' sheds, the Zoma's offerings ranged from refilled Bic lighters and fresh figs to live poultry and intricately embroidered linens. Market stalls were resplendent in the colors of orchids and bird-of-paradise flowers, racks of clothing both old and new, leather and wood carvings, bins of deep yellow, red, and brown spices, carts of dried meats and boxes of delicacies, some for which there seemed to be no name of English equivalence. But whatever the name, if it could be found in Madagascar, the Zoma was sure to carry it.

After the rain, I'd stand on the balcony and listen to the traffic of the Zoma resume its breathless speed — the noise, halted momentarily by the storm, building again until it became a relentless tide spliced now and then by a blast of car horns. Above me, the sky shifted almost imperceptibly from Persian blue to pale blue, sunlight feathered by thin clouds. I watched as the last of the rain, dripping off gutters edging the tiled roof, fell onto the terraced garden that Mme. Arianne, owner of the pension, tended every day. Sometimes after the rain, I'd hear Mme. Arianne playing one of her favorite French ballades, a tune that reminded her, she said, of her university days in Paris. And I'd watch the ever-changing weather and breathe in sugary air scented with orchids and roses.

On the other side of the valley, beyond the Zoma, pink and white stucco buildings nestled along the craggy hills seemed to glow under the sun-washed sky. Only a few buildings were taller than two stories, but stacked against the hillsides, they created the illusion of height. In those first few weeks in Tana while I waited for the paperwork I'd need to begin my research, I had ample opportunity to count the number of tall buildings: the bank, the French-owned department store, two government buildings of plain colonial architecture, all connected to the center of town by the palm-lined boulevard, Avenue de l'Indépendance.

But despite the sprawl of its burgeoning business district, and its ever-growing population of over one million, Tana still had the air of a small town. Given the adobe houses, I could have imagined myself in a coastal town in Mexico, or at an intersection in Ipoh, Malaysia; and if I closed my eyes, I heard the bustle of traffic in New York City or Kingston, Jamaica. But the landscape and the people kept jolting me back to reality. This was Madagascar — modern in its intentions, ancestral in its traditions, moving like the clouds, imperceptibly toward its future while never losing sight of its past.

In those first few weeks in Tana, I set about learning the rhythms of the city. At night, I fell asleep to the yelps of wild dogs quarreling their way through the streets in a language only they understood. Mornings began with the sound of roosters crowing, and the call of the reveille bugle from the army post at the base of the hill. Soon after, I'd hear Teddy, the concierge, unlatching the front gate to the pension. Then the skittering of geckos heading for the shadows of flowerpots, and on the stairstep street outside my shuttered window, the footsteps of passersby so close I almost imagined them, geckos and humans, brushing against the foot of my bed. I listened to the vendors hawk their wares, baskets of bread or fruit, or stacks of firewood on their heads as they climbed the hillside, calling erratically to anyone who might be interested in buying what they had to offer. Sometimes I'd hear Teddy call to one, then a hasty exchange before the vendor moved on up the steps. As the vendors went up the street of stairs, schoolchildren laughed their way down. But some mornings were not so peaceful. Before the vendors and children began passing my window, before the roar of diesel engines from trucks and buses headed for the Zoma, I was jolted awake by the thunder of pestle against mortar as a few hillside residents kept to the old-fashioned practice of pounding coarse grains of rice. Whenever the women lifted the heavy wooden pestles and slammed them into the mortar bowls with cannon fire accuracy, tremors rolled under La Karthala and out toward the Zoma, and I awoke, heart in my throat and convinced that the city was under attack. In response to my call of distress, the family on the terrace directly above the pension moved the time for grain pounding from five a.m. to seven a.m., which allowed me to escape into the madness of city traffic before they began.

All of this made it possible for me to understand the stubbornness of time in a land made famous by lemurs and elephant birds, baobab and tamarind trees, by magnificent comet butterflies with yellow wings that sometimes measured as much as eight inches tip to tip, by chameleons that were all eyes, and walking sticks that measured the length of a schoolchild's ruler—flora and fauna that seemingly had remained unchanged with the passage of centuries. In those first few weeks, with all of the frustrations of bureaucratic red tape, I had a chance to get my bearings in a country that had been both politically and geographically isolated, a place where the past and the present, in all of its extremes, merged into the vividly colorful and sometimes unsettling fabric of the culture. And I learned to come to terms with Tana, with the snail's pace of its business day and the breakneck speed of its traffic.

By the end of my first week in Madagascar, I hired, as Agatha Christie's Hercule Poirot would say, "a guide most excellent." Tiana Flora Tsizaza was a fourth-year student of English literature at the University of Madagascar. She was particularly interested in American literature—everything from *The Great Gatsby* to *The Color Purple* and *The Women of Brewster Place*. For her, the bonus was that I was an African American writer and a professor of literature. For me, the bonus was in having found an assistant who was not only interested in literature but also able to translate from Malagasy and French into English. With Tiana's command of these languages, and her familiarity with a few others that she alluded to but would not claim, we trekked through the maze of government departments for culture and antiquity, the tangle of academic protocol, and the puzzlement of arranging transportation to places where railroads ended and airlines did not venture. The theme song of these offices seemed to be, "Ce n'est pas possible." "This is not possible." But I persisted. Some office calls were made three or four times, until a clerk, catching sight of us again, simply gave in and signed the necessary documents of *les certificats administratifs*. And if we needed duplicates, in Malagasy or French, Tiana copied them right on the spot before the clerk disappeared into the bureaucratic labyrinth and we'd be forced to start again with someone new.

While Tiana translated my intentions to the offices of Recherche et Services des Finances Extérieurs, I tackled the formidable Mme. Bodo of the Agence de Voyages. I mapped out a tentative research itinerary. "I am interested in villages," I told her during the first of many visits. "Places where storytelling is a common occurrence."

Mme. Bodo shrugged her ample shoulders and said, "Possible. Perhaps," in a voice that reminded me of my cousin Anna, who had been a third grade teacher and used the voice of patience as a weapon against even the most truant student. In fact, Mme. Bodo Raobelina looked like my cousin Anna—meticulous and exact behind her night-colored eyes and full lips, round face and soft brown skin, plump fingers that were always counting, counting.

One day, Mme. Bodo turned her patient gaze on me and Tiana. "Are you relatives?" she asked, ticking off the costs of destinations and mileage on her calculator.

Tiana and I looked at each other. There was a similarity in the shape of the face, the nose, the complexion. Could we have had common ancestors? Teddy, the handsome concierge, could have been the brother of one of my classmates at Sumner High School in St. Louis. And surely, someone who looked like Mme. Arianne had sat next to me in a university class in Pennsylvania or Kansas.

"It is possible," Tiana smiled. "Perhaps," I added.

"Do you really think I look Malagasy?" I asked Tiana.

She leaned back and studied me. "Some women in the village where my mother was born braid their hair like yours, but you also look like someone from the South."

I laughed. "I am from the South," I said. "Only the South that I know is thirty thousand miles away from this land." I stared out the window. We were driving along the road outside of Tana heading for a place called Ambohimanga, "the blue mountain." Our guide, Haingolalao, another student at the University of Madagascar and a friend of Tiana's, had promised that at Ambohimanga, I would see the palace of the first king, the birthplace of the Malagasy state. The bustle of Tana had given way to rice fields. In the lemon light of morning, white egrets floated above the young shoots in flooded rice fields, and behind the fields, the hills kept watch. But there was a harsh contrast between the green fields with their flooded dikes, and hillsides scarred from the slash and burn that bared the land for the planting of rice. That was where saplings were gathered to build fires for the rice pots, leaving behind bright gashes of laterite, red and swollen like open wounds, ribboned through the earth. The scene reminded me of the strip-mined hills of Appalachia.

"Is your country very different from this?" Haingo asked.

"In some places," I said. "Although maybe the soil is not so red. Maybe there are not so many villages any more." Already we had passed a half dozen towns, but according to Haingo, we were still some distance away from Ambohimanga.

"The blue mountain is where we have the oldest *rova*," Haingo said. "That is the king's palace, and for the Imerina, it is also the place that once held the ancestral tombs of the royal family. For many years it was forbidden for the people to enter this place without the permission of the king. But now it is a holy city. If we are lucky, we will see those who have come to speak to their ancestors."

To speak to the ancestors, I thought. And I believed that was possible, because the farther we traveled from Tana, the more I felt as if we were traveling into the past. Here and there, towns were cupped in patches of green, but everywhere, there was dust. Perhaps it was the dust that gave me the illusion that I was moving into some ancient time. Dust, churned up by the wheels of the car, blurred the lines between road and field, and the road seemed to undulate, rising from hillsides crevassed with the red scars of erosion, then falling in swirls onto sparse green valleys that I glimpsed only for an instant before the road sent us spiraling onto the next hill.

For miles, ours was the only car on the road, and when we appeared, villagers looked out from their houses like sentries watching us pass. Although there was some distance between villages, there was also a sense of intimacy when we passed through one, the roads so narrow that, if we'd slowed down, I could have shook hands with the people who stood in their doorways to watch us drive by. But their vigil was momentary, because the car whipped through each outpost in almost a blink of the eye—then it was on to the next curve in the road, the next rise of hills, the next town, the car leaving behind it a trail of red dust.

In Tana, I had always been aware of the thin layer of dust that covered everything. At the pension, the wood was polished, the floors scoured with coconut shells, the corners brushed to keep away the dusty pale patina that settled on everything by nightfall. But on the road, the faint red coloring I saw in Tana suddenly took on a deeper shade, staining the countryside between the patches of green with a color that I could scarcely find a name for, a red so vivid that I found myself trying on all the labels I knew: rubia, crimson, cranberry, cinnabar, magenta, mercuro, ocher— and none of them quite right. As we drove along, a comet of red dust whirling behind the car, I hoped that words would not fail me when we reached Ambohimanga.

The road seemed endless, twists and turns through the hills, past rice fields and dikes, and then a swatch of a town that looked like the other towns I'd already seen. Abruptly, the road ended in front of a medieval looking gate. A thatched guard house was perched on the arch of the gate, and pushed to one side was a stone, round as a millstone but so huge, only the gods could have used it for grinding. Haingo told me that the measurement was 4.50 meters, which I calculated to be nearly 15 feet.

"They rolled it over the opening to keep intruders out at night," he said.

"Like a drawbridge," I told him.

The path was steep and wound its way past a few small houses kneeling into the dirt road. Although the houses appeared to be occupied, everyone we met looked like a visitor. "They come from Tana," Haingo said. "And all the towns between."

Tiana recognized a few girls from the University. "Because this is palace of King Andrianampoinimerina, everyone comes to see where he lived," she said. Then, noticing that I was wheezing, she added, "It's very steep, but you can see everything for many, many miles."

I followed her up the slope, and when I reached the first cluster of buildings, sat down on a low wall to catch my breath. Families walked past me—grandfathers leading children, mothers hurrying along beside their mothers, younger sisters with babies on their backs, and lovers, giggling and holding hands. A group of musicians walked by, carrying trumpets, guitars, and *valihas* made from beautifully carved bamboo, strips of the wood cut away to form a circle of strings, like a harp, around a tube of wood. I had heard the sound of the *valiha* only once before, at a concert played by Rossy in the U.S. I found its music so hauntingly beautiful, I would never forget it. They all moved briskly, making me grow even more impatient with my faulty breathing. Then I noticed a group working its way up the path at an even slower pace than I had managed. From a distance, they were so tightly clustered together, they seemed to be marching in slow motion. The men were wearing red and white lambas tied over their trousers. "The lambas have the pattern of a nearby village," Tiana said. It was only when they came closer that I noticed they seemed to be supporting two older people in the middle of the group who were moving so slowly, I thought at first that they were being carried.

"They have come to consult with the ancestors," Tiana said. "Maybe someone is sick or someone is in need of money. In the *rova*, they will find a person who speaks in the voice of the ancestors."

"Like an oracle?" I asked.

"No, it is the ancestor who speaks," she said.

"That is what we believe," Haingo said.

We moved past the group and on up the slope. I made the rest of the climb effortlessly, and when I reached the square at the top of the slope, I saw the musicians, who'd been climbing up the hill a few moments earlier, setting up their chairs on a small stage. In the middle of the square, children played tag, and their parents strolled around the edges of the square. The terrace of a restaurant at the opposite end of the square was already crowded. (Later, I would discover that behind this restaurant was an outdoor privy unique to Madagascar: two turtle shells placed on either side of the hole. And there, I also discovered that my balance was much better than my breathing.) Across from the restaurant was a set of wide stone stairs with a constant stream of people moving up and down them.

"That is the *rova*," Haingo said.

I spotted the red and white lambas inching up the steps. "They will have some ritual up there," Tiana said.

"Will they let me watch?" I asked.

But Haingo was already leading the way up the steps. I loosened the case on my camera, and told myself to remember everything.

There was much to remember. I joined the procession of people walking through the *rova*: the quiet rooms of the palace, the king's bed with a trundle for his favorite wife, the regalia of kings and queens displayed in a collection that ranged from large carved bowls to weapons. This place of royalty had held over a century of rulers from King Andrianampoinimerina to Queen Ranavalona III, the last monarch of Madagascar. There, in the half dark, the past seemed real to me. This must be how the ancestors speak to the people, I thought, but then, I was a *vazaha*, a foreigner who was accustomed to the Western ideas of the division between life and death. I could not know the ways of ancestors. I had to remind myself that I was in a country where the dead were still living, where spirits were not ghosts but the *fanahy*, where the line between life and death was not circumscribed by a physical presence, and where the wisdom of ancestors, the *razana*, could be imparted to the living.

When we left the palace, a crowd had already gathered in the king's garden. I jockeyed my way into place beside a Flaming Katy bush. I had a limited view, but I could still see the clearing, a smooth rock area behind the walls of the palace that, I was told, had been the bathing place of the king. I saw the men in the red and white lambas standing in a sort of semicircle—three younger men and one very old man who seemed scarcely able to walk. One of the men, in a red watchcap, stood a little bit apart from the group. He seemed to be the leader, the orator. The old woman stood nearby, her gray head bent as she listened. There was a ceremony, the sacrifice of a chicken, the call to enter *tanin-dolo*, the spirit realm.

"They will see if the omens are right," Tiana said. "The woman is asking for some advice, and they will listen to what the ancestors say. If it will be wise for her to do this or to do that."

While the men were engrossed in the ceremony, the crowd shifted—people moving forward to see the sacrificed chicken; people moving closer to get a better view of the orator; children darting about, listening open-mouthed, then running off to explore some other place. Aside from those involved in the ceremony, there seemed to be no function for onlookers, and aside from the lambas, there seemed to be no special dress. Hesitantly at first, I began to take pictures. One of the men caught the glint of light off the camera lens, looked my way, and smiled. I took several more shots. One man would talk, then another. The old woman tightened the white lamba around her shoulders and nodded that she understood. Then, by some tacit agreement that I didn't understand, it was over.

"Now they will go to the sacred place," Haingo said.

I followed the crowd up the final slope. It was a curious procession, serious, yet no one seemed to be in a hurry. The old man moved slowly but steadily up the rise. Young couples joined us, drawn away from the musicians in the square. I was just beginning to hear the first strains of their music. Everyone's mood seemed to have lightened once we passed the sacrificial place, but still, I wasn't prepared for what I saw at the clearing. The view was spectacular, an expanse of land that, after the closeness of the courtyard, seemed to go on forever. The clearing was an outcrop of stone wedding the valley below to the sky above. Over the lip of stone, about a hundred feet down, a panoramic landscape stretched in an endless pattern of hills and valleys, swampy cuts of rice fields connecting brown hills stippled with bright red smudges of erosion, a land so occu-

pied with its past that it needed only a nudge to loosen its topsoil and ex-
pose its beginnings. *Tanindrazana*, land of the ancestors, it was called,
and from the crest of the "blue mountain," I could see why. I moved close
enough to the edge to see the highway, twisting like a liana vine into the
hills, miniature villages strung like worry beads along the edge of the
road. At this height above the valley, the wind was clear, and dust seemed
a distant thing that I had imagined. But it wasn't so much the sense of
height—I'd been to mountains that were profoundly higher—but the
sense of space, the suddenness of open air without the obstruction of
buildings, cattle, and from this distance, even people. Yet unlike the
young girls sitting on the rim of the shelf, swinging their legs as if they
were sitting on the front porch of a house in the city, no matter how
much Haingo urged me, I avoided walking to the edge where I could
look down at the valley from a dizzying height. Instead, I claimed to be
studying the markings on the stone shelf: two uneven circles, a white one
nested inside a larger red one. "Red is the blood of the people, of the
land," Tiana said. "And white is for the bones of the ancestors."

I began to focus my camera. Then, in the corner of the lens, I saw the
old man moving toward the center of the circle. In the palace garden, he'd
walked with a cane, his steps so small he'd seemed to be creeping forward.
Now, the cane seemed no more than a decoration, a prop that added experience to his years. Instead of bending over in the turtle hump of the
very elderly, he stood erect, and his step was smooth. He danced, that old
man turned young. While the wind blowing off the basin ruffled the
skirts of the young girls sitting on the edge of the rock, the old man beseeched the ancestors with a dance of lamentation and laughter from the
living. He danced without regard to the precipice a few yards from his
feet, or the girls who giggled behind their cupped hands, or the young
men who kept time by clapping, or the children who imitated his steps
from a safe distance. It was a dance of incantation, a dance of reverence, a
dance that for the Malagasy was part of the natural order of life. I thought
he danced without music until I realized that the music he listened to

had been played years ago, on this very same spot, by those who were now called *razana*. Off to one side, the old woman who had come to hear the wisdom of the dead was smiling. I began to think that I was the only one who found this incredible—the dance, the expanse of land, the old man who no longer seemed old. I had much to learn from an island of stone, an island of soil red as blood, an island of ancestors and stories that were told and retold through countless generations.

Several weeks later, at the Musée d'Art et d'Archeologie in Antananarivo, I spoke with the archivist, M. Alphonse Raharison, about the importance of ancestors in shaping the stories of the oral tradition. "Are the ancestors a spiritual force for the Malagasy people?" I asked.

"We do not worship the ancestors, but we look to them for wisdom," he said. "It is what we call *Kohèfy manàra-panjatra*—as the thread follows the needle. Even for scholars, this is true."

He took me through the museum, which was housed in a French colonial villa in Isoraka, an Upper Town region of Tana. Each room held specific artifacts of Malagasy history and culture: lambas, woven hats, and wall hangings from many regions of the country; carved *aloalo* tomb markings from the coastal regions, antique boards for games of *fanorona*, musical instruments, photographs, and of course, manuscripts written in *sora be*, a script similar to Arabic. The past dominated everything, and the presence of the French seemed to be a mere coincidence.

"We have set about to collect a proper history of the Malagasy people," M. Raharison said. "Scholars from all over Madagascar are contributing to our archives. It is very important that we have access to our own stories."

That night, as I fell asleep, I heard the wild dogs begin their serenade. Random at first, a single bark or so, then three or four, and finally a chorus of challenges and agreements. They stayed in the hills until some time after midnight, their signals getting louder, more frantic, until by some secret code, they descended into the city. I heard them scrambling like greyhounds past my bedroom window, snarls and muffled growls marking their descent down the stairs. They raced past, claws clicking against stone, snarling and growling, pausing to settle arguments, unruly but so close I could almost count them — ten, twenty, and from what I imagined behind the safe shutters of my window, each smelly with wild, rancid breath. I heard them trailing through the market, cutting back, running, running up another stairway street perhaps, muffled growls growing fainter until finally a lone bark or two echoed once more from the hills. Then quiet descended on the city, the calm before morning, the next few hours interrupted only by the click of geckos, or the sweet call of a night bird singing to all the towns between the ancestors and earth.

ഗ്രഗ്രഗ്രഗ്രഗ്രഗ്രഗ്രഗ്രഗ്രഗ്രഗ്രഗ്രഗ്രഗ്രഗ്ര

HOW STORIES CAME TO BE: THREE VIEWS

Origins of Myths: from M. Alphonse Raharison —
archivist, Musée d'Art et d'Archeologie, Antananarivo

The myths of Madagascar originate with Zanahary (God). When Zanahary created the people from dust, He also created the stories that would help the people understand life. One kind of story, or *angano*, that He created was the tales about daily life, the social life of the people. These tales were told by the old people, and later recounted by the scholars and linguists. The purpose of these tales is to educate the people: to show them how to respect the social structure, to show the women how to behave in the family's life, to describe who is responsible for domestic work, and to tell the women how they should obey.

These tales are told so that the people will know how children speak to their elders, or how children speak before women, or when women can speak. We have a saying in Madagascar, *Ny zaza am-behi-vavy* — "The children and the women," which shows the importance of social order. But this social order is not as difficult in Madagascar as it might be in the West. For example, the king, Andrianampoinimerina, was put on the throne by his grandmother. This was the way of choosing the king until the nineteenth century. In the West, the king is chosen from the next male heir to the throne, unless the king does not leave a son, then the throne goes to the queen. But until the nineteenth century, the king was chosen by the grandmother, which was the social order for that period and told in the stories about the king.

There are also other stories, such as the origins of some facts. The tales known as *arira*, about the animals, recall, for example, why it is that dogs chase cats. The stories tell about how the dogs remember what the cats did to betray them, and to this day they still chase them in anger. There are also *tantara*, legends about clever creatures, such as "Ikely Mahitisy," the little boy who is a trickster. He is very clever, and if someone does something to him, he finds a way to get back at them. He is invisible to the people, but they know he is there to remind them how to behave. He can manipulate them, and he always gets away with his tricks. And there are tales about those who are handicapped, such as "Just Head," who is not strong, but he is able to make the people see how they should behave. The storyteller must be careful not to tell these stories every day for fear some malady will befall the people because these tricksters now have a voice.

Some stories recount how tribes or villages came to be named as they are. For example, Masikoro is a name given to the people of the southern interior who are farmers. Their stories are about the spirits of the wheat fields and the rice fields. But the stories of their neighbors, the Vezo who live on the southwestern coast, are about the sea, because the Vezo are seagoing fishermen. These stories tell about the origins of why the people fish or plant the crops of the fields. Many stories are to show how the people must respect what we call *fihavanana*, blood relations or close friendships, friends who are like family. These stories are special to the ancestors and to the old people. They tell us about our roles in society. Sometimes the orator at circumcisions and exhumations will tell stories about *fihavanana* also.

Many say that the stories are an obstacle to the politics of modernization. It is true that modernization may mean eliminating the myths and stories of the oral tradition. It is necessary but not equal to modernization to help the people not be afraid of the future. But the people are afraid of letting go of the stories because they are reluctant to change, contrary to the politicians who want change. So there is the conflict. It is the oral tradition that helps make for the harmony of life, and the need for literacy that will take us into the modern future.

ை‌ை‌ை‌ை‌ை

Tapasiry—Tales from the South:
from Professor Aurélien de Moussa Behavira, University of Toliara

There are many kinds of stories and ceremonies. In Toliara, the story is called *tapasiry*; in Fort Dauphin, it is called *takasiry*; and the Tanosy call the short tales *tapasiry fohy*, or *tapatono*. Many rituals are connected to these stories. Some stories are told in the *sarandra*, or the song. This telling of stories in song comes from the idea that when cowherds whistle, the echo extends for some distance. The echo is like the response that the audience gives the song.

Among the Tanosy, the Antanosy group of the southern part of Madagascar, the art of healing, or *fanaoana hazomanga*, is performed to rid people of evil spirits, called *tromba*. In the South, this art of healing is important to help people who are under the divine possession, called *bilo kitonotono*. The *hazomanga*, the sacred wood, comes from the legend about God's daughter, who died and in whose place there grew a great tree which was blessed with healing powers and could soothe those who were troubled. This sacred wood has two functions: in the South, it is used for

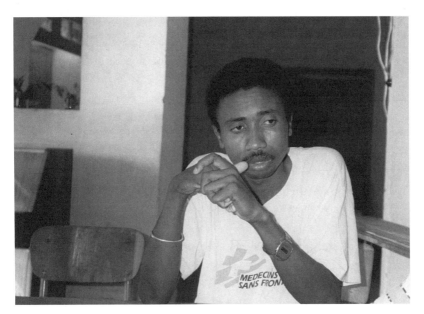

Professor Aurélien de Moussa Behavira, University of Toliara

healing; among the Betsileo, it is a sacred gift from God. In the South, it is a huge tree kept outside the house; when it is used by the Betsileo, it is a piece of wood kept inside the house.

The *sarandra* is a type of song used at funerals and in ceremonies that tell the people how they must live. Among the Tanosy, the *sarandra* is a story, the story of the dead performed at a funeral and told through a song. When the griot performs the song, the audience responds, as in a call/response song. The *sarandra* tells about the person, and is sent to the ancestor to say that the one who has died is coming.

When there is a marriage, the parents of the couple must consult the diviner, who will then choose the most auspicious day for the ceremony. This ritual is the *sahiry*, and the diviner acts as if he is the artist that makes the marriage. The parents are the owners of the marriage but the diviner makes the prediction for the marriage.

A ceremony, *jihe*, can be for marriage or blessing the young. The *fanindrahindrana*, a praise or blessing of the young, will be performed as a chant for ten to fifty children. The circumcision ceremony for boys, *famorana*, is performed every seven years in the South. These ceremonies differ from the entreaty or prayer to the ancestor or God. The entreaty, *takasy*, is a song practiced by the conjuror: called *masy* for the female, and *miha* for the male.

One type of song that is based on legend is the *takasiry*, which is told to educate the people as to their responsibilities and how they should live. For example, there are songs that tell stories about the disobedient child, or about the lazy villager who does not want to work the field. And there is a song that is performed to scare the woman who does not want to marry an ordinary village man. The storyteller improvises the story so the women who are listening hear what happens when this woman is tricked into marrying a monster. Sometimes a song is added to the story so that the audience won't be bored.

Another *sarandra* is a lively song performed by the Tanosy that tells the people how to live. The story can vary between one cultural group and another, although there may be a similar song about the genealogy of cultural life. The melodies vary, and there are many metaphors about the circumstances of marriage or circumcision based on the astrology of the diviner. These metaphors are for the honor of the families. In circumcision, the metaphors present a challenge to the mother's brother, because it is the uncle who would bear the blame if the child is unable to withstand the circumcision. The uncle makes a torch from the *hazo-manga*, the wood used for the fire of circumcision, and accepts the challenge by representing the mother at the ceremony. There is a type of song used at circumcision to give strength and bravery, for example:

boys
only children make animals of clay
they make them fight
that animal (how strong)

to whom does the most powerful belong
ours
beast of a man (a wild cat of a man)
so strong not even the blade defeats him

സൈസൈസൈസൈസൈ

The Oral Tradition: from Ernest Rakotosalama, poet, Fianarantsoa

In the early days, not all of the Malagasy were able to write. At first, many people only used the stories told in the oral tradition. The writing came from these stories. Early writing, *sora be*, was from Arabic script, but always the stories were honored. Nothing was direct. The people didn't like to be offensive, so they used indirect ways of speaking—turns of speech—and in that way, held respect for each other. They did not like to interrupt the speaker. There is a proverb that says: To interrupt some-one is like interrupting breath. The people in relationships knew the stories were important because they could use these stories to reach each other. And so, over the years, the stories were brought over the mountains and rivers throughout Madagascar.

In the early days, there was a limit to how people could regard each other, but everyone needed the king and the king needed the people. As the say-ing goes: The king does not rule without the people. This means that the people created the king, the king did not create the people. Those who send for the king will grow fat, but if the king cannot be sent for, there is no need to have a king. To be able to send for the king means that you are prosperous because of what the king will give you. Daily work is also important to understanding the stories. Again, the proverb says: The one that leads the pack of wild boars knows the usual road. That means that those who are experienced can lead those who do not have experi-ence. The stories of the people emerged from their surroundings, from what was as natural as drawing water from the well. Stories were told to entertain and designed to help people remember them. The stories that were repeated often were the ones that people could remember. The people will ponder upon the morals of these stories.

Many stories were lost during colonial times, because the Malagasy people were not instructed in the Malagasy language. The missionaries changed the authentic literature to the foreign literature. They believed that the stories were a way of worshiping idols. It is still true that storytellers will not tell stories unless they trust you. Poems, like some stories, are not told directly. The poem, *tango haro*, was made from not one idea but many images that come from different parts of a life, like pulling the wings, legs, and head off a captive grasshopper. This is one of the metaphors the people use to explain life.

CHAPTER II

UNDER SOUTHERN SKIES
Memoirs of Toliara

When we stepped from the plane in Toliara, we were greeted by a dense heat usually associated with humid tropical climates, but according to the weather charts, we had arrived in the dry season. It took only a few minutes to realize that the humidity was deceptive, that in fact the hot air was stirred by wind and dust, and the bright sunlight was barely tempered by breezes blowing offshore from the Mozambique Channel. On the southern coast, the heat begins inland, undulating in almost visible waves across the great spiny forest, so named because of the treetop tall cacti standing guard over sisal, baobabs, and termite anthills, cones of clay rising two or three feet high and clustered like condos in a suburb. I had passed half a dozen sets of those clay towers before I realized they were the work of insects and not eruptions of small volcanos left by natural shifts in desert soil. At first glance, they resembled smaller versions of the rock sculptures in the Isalo massifs, a national park area located a few hundred miles north of Toliara. The labyrinthine sandstones in Isalo have been scoured by wind, each mysterious shape seeming to echo Madagascar's murky past, suggesting columns, walls, and avenues where kings may have once reigned before centuries of hot desert winds took their toll. But unlike Isalo with its moonscape of craters and monoliths, the termite cones stand guard where cacti have given way to sisal fields, the plants stretching in endless logarithms toward the horizon in one direction, and the Mozambique Channel in the other. And nestled in a bay leading to the channel: Toliara.

On the southern coast, the soil is dry and sandy, and palm trees bend under the brisk coastal breezes. This was my first sense of the region: heat, dust, and the wind. While the station wagon transporting me and Tiana from the airport to the Villa Plaza sped toward town, I looked behind us to see dust swirling along the road, sometimes all but hiding the retreating figure of a passerby shimmering in an updraft of heat. Dust cloaked fig, tamarind, and mango trees, coated the leaves of aloe and periwinkle, the bright red petals of Flaming Katy and heavily scented jasmine. In town, dust eroded the sidewalks until the low stone fences surrounding colonial villas left no demarcation between land and road.

The town of Toliara held echoes of the colonial French the way a seashell holds the sound of oceans. Up close, the French presence was obvious, but turn your head slightly and the impression faded, their ghosts held in check by descendants of revolutionary Malagasy who had routed the French in a bloody fight for independence over thirty years ago. Half the French-style villas in Toliara were spacious houses partially hidden by garden walls, and slumbering in disrepair. But in all of Toliara, the colonial past was a mere whisper in the town's attendance to government business, the tourist trade, and weighing the harvest of the ocean. On the main street, the open air market thrived with the comings and goings of housewives, schoolchildren, and university students. The day we arrived, the university was on strike and students blocked the school's doorways in protest over the conditions there. Other parts of town kept to the usual rhythms of daily life. The men refrained from entering the market where most of the vendors and buyers were women, but groups of men, in their idle hours, gathered on nearby front stoops or under the shade of a *kily* tree for one or two rounds of the ancient game of *fanorona*, moving pebbles across the gameboard like chess players.

Along the shore, the Malagasy morning was clocked by women bringing in baskets of shellfish, their work as brisk and important as the
sunrise. Evening hours were marked by raucous young boys gleefully
bathing in the surf, their nude bodies glistening like fish as they leapt
among the waves. But always there was the sea breaking cool and foamy
at the end of *kily*-lined thoroughfares leading to the ocean; and in beach-
front villas, similar to the one Tiana and I had checked into for the du-
ration of our stay, the days hummed along with the efficiency of any
resort. The concierge, a French expatriate, busied herself with linens and
silverware, lawns and umbrellas, and the mundane routine of running a
hotel, while the land and sea kept to its own time schedule of tides, sands,
and a host of insects—"critters" we called them back home.

On the southern coast, the sea takes its own level, cutting a corrugated
shoreline of reefs and eddies into the sometimes shallow, sometimes deep
waters. There is nothing beyond except Antarctica. At Cap Sainte Marie,
a sign warns: "Stop! Extreme South!" Beyond it, the ocean goes on forever. These rocky shores have kept safe a landscape that seems pulled
from another time.

That landscape made it clear why the island had been nicknamed
"The Land That Time Forgot." In the southern region, near Isalo, ex-
plorers still found the giant eggs of the roc, the great elephant bird, while
the tiny mouse lemur and Brookesia chameleon, small as a thumbnail,
lived in the leaf shade of the rain forest among the pitcher plants and
bottle trees. In town, insects screamed warnings from deep shadows of
mangroves morning to evening, and nights were filled with the chitter-
ings of hissing cockroaches, gathered like gangsters under the haloes of
street lights. One morning, I awoke to find several of them making themselves at home in my hair. They were as big as half-dollars, metallic black
creepy crawlies from the Ice Age. They were Rambo-sized pterodactyls
of the insect world, their grip on my hair as tight as any championship
wrestler's. When I slapped my braids to shake them loose, they chittered

like cartoon characters. I nearly went into convulsions, jerking myself around in bizarre arabesques punctuated by screams and a rapid flapping of my arms. Tiana entered my room to find me stark naked, yelling: "KILL THEM! KILL THEM!" So much for the austere Fulbright scholar maintaining a proper distance from her translator. I'm sure that was the incident that helped Tiana and me become close friends.

To get through the heart of town to the suburbs where the Ministry of Culture was located, we took a pousse-pousse, one of the Malagasy rickshaws that along with bicycles created more congestion than the cars and the few buses that were routed through Toliara. The drivers were sinewy and athletic, their bodies toned by running, usually barefoot, as they pulled their carriages behind them. They had feet of beautiful proportions, so well articulated that Michelangelo would have given them to David had he chosen a Malagasy for his model. But these models were mere mortals, and clamored for fares just as aggressively as any stateside cabbie.

Tiana and I had to run the gamut of pousse-pousse carriages lined up in front of our hotel like hansom cabs or New York taxis, but the hassle was well worth it. It was a chance to see the town unfold at a less hectic pace than in some car turned taxi that might break down at the next corner. The pousse-pousse carried us along the wide, tree-lined main street and turned inland from the coast. We passed children riding in a school-bound pousse-pousse in the opposite direction, and women setting out on errands, their postures lending a straight line of definition to the shallow curve of the pousse-pousse. We passed the market where vendors were arranging baskets of red ripe tomatoes next to baskets of wild yams, or hanging lambas from wires across the front of their stalls, swatches of cloth fluttering like bright flower petals. We maneuvered through a traffic jam of freight-bound pousse-pousses swaying past office-bound carriages. Our driver pulled us swiftly through the middle of town, his pace as sure as an Olympic runner's. He did not slow his step until we reached an area of government buildings, converted villas set away from the

Willy Marcel, Cultural Minister, Toliara

street by low fences or border hedges, a small sign half hidden somewhere near the entrance to designate the Office of Cultural Affairs.

Our contact was Willy Marcel, the Cultural Minister. I waited on the
portico while Tiana assured a clerk that indeed we had an appointment.
Through a window, I could see a wall covered with maps and several
glassed-in display cases. This contrasted sharply with the scene outside,
where chickens clucked at the dirt and the caretaker's family went about
their morning chores in front of a lean-to at the far end of the yard, where
a couple of goats were tethered.

None of that surprised me, for despite the lingering traces of the
French and the resort atmosphere of the seaside hotels, Toliara was more
rural than urban, a fishing town perched at the edge of sisal fields. But
like most coastal towns in Madagascar, Toliara was still dependent on the

sea, its commerce a blend of tradition and emerging technology. This was a common situation in Madagascar. In Toliara, fishermen still cast nets from pirogues, and freshly dyed fabrics were left on rough-made looms to dry in the sun, while Japanese businessmen arranged tariffs for exporting Malagasy goods. In the capital city of Tana, I had seen office workers in suits, briefcases in hand, walking across the dikes of flooded rice fields to bus stops on the highway, their figures silhouetted like commuters against the late summer sky. But what puzzled me at the Ministry of Culture was an old French car parked in the crook of the portico, not an inch to spare around it, and from my estimation, a wheelbase that was at least a smidgen wider than the concrete railing lining the portico stairs. Did someone bring the car onto the veranda piece by piece? Did they haul it up and over and sideways? I never uncovered the method. When I asked how the car had arrived at its permanent nesting place, Willy Marcel proved to be as elusive as he was friendly. Instead of an answer, I received a cup of sugary Malagasy tea and a tour of the government's ethnographic museum.

As I besieged M. Marcel with my midwestern tone-deaf version of French, he labored through classroom English. I asked about his life in Toliara, the responsibilities of being a government official, and if there was any real evidence of the pirate ships that were said to have landed on the coast long ago. He asked me if I knew about Michael Jackson, Whitney Houston, and "beautiful American women who spend all day lying in the sun." At the end of each question, he smiled and winked, a wonderful spiderwebbing of laugh-lines appearing around his eyes. He recited an English language poem he'd learned in school. I tried to remember some clever French phrase of equal literary quality, but the moment passed and Tiana was left struggling to keep a straight face while she translated for both of us. At one point, she whispered, "Ce n'est pas possible," but I dismissed her pessimism with a wave of my hand. I knew that Willy Marcel and I were fated to communicate, at the expense of both languages if need be.

Having been dispatched from the capital city to the government post

Aloalo carving from Toliara

in Toliara, Monsieur Marcel was determined to prove his worth so that
fortune would see him sent back to the capital, "Where I am needed," he
smiled. "Here I am a waste," he added, gesturing to the dungeon-like
confines of his office, the disheveled mass of ribbon-tied files in the ad-
joining room, and the crumbling stone portico and dirt courtyard beyond.
Over cups of Malagasy tea, Willy Marcel discussed the difficulties of han-
dling the affairs of several tribal cultures, all placed under the control of
the central government in Tana. "Art is very important to each culture,"
he said. "It is tradition." He showed me the Ministry's collection of *aloalo*,
tomb markings sculpted from *hazomanga*, a sacred wood full of light
sworls, and the darker varieties that had been seasoned in the rice fields.
      Later, after Tiana and I had left Toliara, I would see other examples
of *aloalo*: some quite ordinary depictions of the riches of an ancestor's
time on earth—cattle, soldiers, boats and planes—and some more ex-

plicitly erotic, marking the death of a virile man or, in the distant past, a man with many wives — sensual bodies enhanced by the sheen of the wood, male and female figures, more regal than lascivious, blissfully aloof from anything but their union. But in Toliara, in Willy Marcel's office, I examined at close hand an *aloalo* that depicted two men slaughtering a zebu. It was a magnificent carving in which both men and beast seemed to be rising away from the wood. Willy Marcel's tone turned serious when he explained the *aloalo*.

"This tells the stories of the ancestors," he said. "This says that with the sacrifice of the zebu there will be a feast, and the wealth of the man who has been owning the zebu will be the wealth of the village." He said that like *fitenin-drazana*, the words of the ancestors, these carvings linked the dead with the living. He used a large map to show me in which district the carving had been made, and how the details and sworls of wood held their own stories. Once he understood my genuine interest, Willy Marcel stopped making references to pop singers and "beautiful American women who spend all day lying in the sun." We struck a deal, Willy Marcel and I. And in the end, it was a fair trade. In exchange for the myths of American pop culture, he told me the stories of the peoples of the high plateau region of Madagascar: the Merina and Bara and Mahafaly. Before the visit was over, he arranged a meeting with storytellers and musicians from surrounding villages. And it was then, on the third day of my visit to Toliara, that I entered the world of myth and realism on the portico of the Minister of Culture.

Tiana and I arrived early, but that day in the courtyard of the Cultural Ministry, time slipped into coincidence and turned fluid. That morning, the courtyard held a flurry of activity. The chickens had retreated into a corner under a *kily* tree, and the goats eyed us with amusement. Monsieur Marcel had sent his assistants to contact storytellers in several villages. Having done so, he left Tiana and me to our own devices of language and cameras. Waiting for us on the portico was a dance troupe

With the Manindry Dance Troupe, Toliara

and an accomplished *mpikabary*, an experienced man of words. But it was the musicians who first brought the neighborhood children into the courtyard. They appeared as if by magic or by the secret ear that children tune to the call of music and stories. I could hardly blame them. Once the Manindry dance troupe arranged themselves on the portico, they held everyone's attention. The troupe was composed of five women and a man, the lead musician, from a village a few miles from the far edge of Toliara. Wearing a Guinness Stout T-shirt, a lamba, and his hair in short dreadlocks, the leader was a handsome young man with perfectly articulated feet—another artist's model, I was sure. He played a stringed instrument, a cross between a fiddle and a ukelele, a squarish

Drummer, Manindry dance troupe, Toliara

box that he bowed like a Stradivarius and with the skill of any classical musician. That and the drum were the troupe's only instruments. The rest was voice and dance, performed by women who seemed to me, the outsider, to be both fragile and resilient. Like the leader, they wore lambas and short-sleeved shirts, but they also wore the traditional round, brimless straw hat, squared at the crown with red bark dye patterned in the woven sisal.

Before each piece began, the leader rushed about, ordering the group into position with the insistence of a stage director. The women waited with the easy poise of seasoned performers, but once the drummer, a round-faced woman with delicate looking hands, signaled the rhythm, they were commanded by the story. On that crowded portico, on the other side of the flimsy barrier separating the abandoned French car from the dancers and the clusters of neighborhood children, the Manindry troupe offered tales of myth and origin, *sarandra* that have evolved through generations of Malagasy storytellers, each song-poem accompanied by a dance where one movement of the body — the way the head turned, the arch of the hand, or the quickening of breath — flowed into the next. Each movement symbolized some aspect of the story, the dance taking on the storyteller's task of a change in voice or intonation, a shift in mood or perspective: one posture suggesting the bravery of a warrior, another the fate of star-crossed lovers, or the temptation of a water spirit, a Lorelei who lures the prince to follow her into the ocean's depths by swinging her lustrous hair. But the prince dances away on wondrous feet, while the group's drummer counts out the pulse of prince and temptress both. The Manindry's performance was an excellent complement to the *angano*, the oral tales of Madagascar, but despite all the flash of strings and drums, it was Monsieur Soaraza's talk-stories that held the children entranced.

When he arrived, one of Monsieur Marcel's assistants brought out a chair for him, and enthroned in the center of the portico, Monsieur Soaraza waited until the Manindry troupe finished performing. At times, I thought he'd fallen asleep. But when the dancers' song-poem depicted something humorous, he laughed along with the rest of us. And when Tiana introduced us, I saw from his expression that he'd been watching me as much as I had been watching him. Accompanied by a young boy — his great grandson I was told — he had walked to Toliara from a village several kilometers away, along hill country roads best suited to goats and

Storyteller, M. Soaraza, Toliara

children. But Monsieur Soaraza, hardly a child, must have been at least eight decades older than the boy who had accompanied him. I have in my living room a carving of an African griot, a gaunt man with high cheekbones and sinewy muscles—a storyteller's staff in one hand, one shoulder cloaked in patterned cloth and the other bare. Monsieur Soaraza, a bright green lamba draped over one shoulder and a walking stick to aid his failing eyesight, could have posed for such a carving. His distinctive African features set him apart from the Merina and Betsileo groups of the high plateau country. His body was thin and wiry, his face angular. He could have been Bara, Mahafaly, or Makoa with his angular face, and the deep walnut hues of his skin. The face of a griot, I told myself. And if I had even the slightest doubt about Monsieur Soaraza's skills as a storyteller, he put them to rest with the telling of his first tale.

For more than an hour, we listened as he told one tale after another: the *tapasiry*, tales of social conduct, and the *tantara*, myths of origins. While those stories unfolded, a rooster inexplicably crowed from time to time as if recalling the pleasure of hearing those same stories in another courtyard with another storyteller. But it was all quite logical: the rooster's crowing, the stories woven from oral tradition, the children listening with rapt attention to tales that had been told and retold over the centuries. That's the way it was in Madagascar—the past meeting the present in unexpected places. While we listened, I watched the young boy who had accompanied Monsieur Soaraza. He listened intently as if each *angano*, each story, held for him the magic of its first telling. I have rarely seen a storyteller's apprentice, but I swear, that boy's face held the tracings of that ancient vocation. Throughout the telling, Monsieur Soaraza and the boy seemed to be locked in some special time and place where legends are alive and evolving. Not even the clicking of my camera could break that spell. Behind them, the neighborhood children were transfixed as the stories turned into a play of light and shadows, and Monsieur Soaraza's elegant gestures brought the legends onto the portico of the Cultural Minister, holding them there like the old French car—seemingly too wide to be contained in such a small space, and almost too enigmatic to be explained. These tales, as told to me, are those I relate to you now.

Azonay Tsy Avelanay
If we have it, don't lose it.
MALAGASY PROVERB

শ্রীশ্রীশ্রীশ্রীশ্রী

Papango Fito Loha: Seven-headed Hawk

It had seven heads. This one thing had seven heads. It had killed his father . . . the father of Tsimamanga. It was said that the father of Tsimamanga was killed by Papango Fito Loha, the Seven-headed Hawk, when he bathed. At his birth, Tsimamanga was left behind by his mother who had been taken away, taken away by Papango Fito Loha, the Seven-headed Hawk. He was there. So what? Yes, he grew up. And when he grew up, what he did was to go away, because as a child he had always heard the questions: "Where is that child's mother? Where is that child's father?"

"I don't know that," he had answered. "I don't know that. But tell me, if he is not dead, where is my father? Tell me," Tsimamanga said.

"Your father," the gossip ran, "was killed by Papango Fito Loha, and is dead over there. Your mother was taken away, taken away by Papango Fito Loha. She is dead in the ocean, over there, out of sight."

"Is that what has happened to my mother, to my father?"

"Yes," the rumors were told. So Tsimamanga left. And when he left, he took with him a stick made of gold and *vohipoy*, which is a kind of tree. The ocean was immense and consumed the whole world; it seemed to be endless. So Tsimamanga said, "What will I do with this?"

"Blow on me seven times," the ocean said.

And Tisimamanga blew on it seven times; he blew on it seven times. And the ocean drew back; the ocean drew back. And that is when he saw a monster.

"How are you doing, Monster?" he said. The monster was a whale, an enormous whale living in the ocean, a dragon whale. "Carry me on your back to cross over there," he asked. And Tsimamanga was carried on its back, carried on its back, carried on its back. While the Monster whale carried him on its back, and it went out so far, so far, it said, "This is not my land anymore, but Ndrimobe's." And the dragon whale died.

And then, Ndrimobe carried him on its back. Tsimamanga was carried on its back, carried on its back, carried on its back. Ndrimobe dropped him off a crevasse, on ground that was eaten away and cracked. The land was so cracked that if anyone fell down into it, an animal would eat them up. It was gravelly ground, hard to step on. It was uneven ground.

"What am I going to do with this ground?" Tsimamanga thought. "I can't walk on this ground."

Then there appeared Karakara Fito, the one who tends the thing with seven heads. Karakara Fito was a friend of Papango Fito Loha. Yes, Karakara Fito was its amulet, its guardian. But Tsimamanga's amulet was Valamangatsiritra. So when he asked, "Valamangatsiritra, what do we do with this ocean?" Valamangatsiritra would make the ocean say, "Blow the wind on me seven times." And then the ocean would draw back. So now, Tsimamanga had to step on that dangerous crevasse. "What should I do with this ground?" Tsimamanga asked.

"Blow air on me seven times," Valamangatsiritra said.

And the gravel disappeared and grew loamy, easy to step on. And Tsimamanga crossed. He walked and he walked and happened upon a very fierce animal, called Menarana (a serpent of the boa kind). No one had ever been able to come close to Menarana. Tsimamanga was terrified.

"What will I do with this?" he asked Valamangatsiritra.

"Point me to its direction seven times," Valamangatsiritra said. He pointed Valamangatsiritra in the direction of the animal, and Menarana, the Serpent, was defeated and became tame.

Tsimamanga walked a little further, and saw a river. Papango Fito Loha dwelt in the giant tamarind tree by the river. Rumor said that he dwelt in that tree. A few children came to fetch water. When Tsimamanga saw them, he was furious with them because he knew the river was where his parents were killed by Papango Fito Loha. He said to the children, "How dare you fetch water in the place where my father and mother were killed by that animal." And he grabbed all of their watering jugs and broke them.

Now Papango Fito Loha was up there in the tamarind tree and he saw everything. He saw the children go back home. There, their parents asked, "Where are your watering jugs?"

"We left them behind," the children said. And Papango Fito Loha saw them stay in their houses.

At that moment, the creature Zaraniahitry, he who divides the weeds, came to fetch water in that same river. Tsimamanga was furious and when he took Zaraniahitry, he grabbed him and swung him and swung him. Then he put a spell on Zaraniahitry with his amulet, Valamangatsiritra. Valamangatsiritra put a spell, put a spell, and Zaraniahitry was stunned.

Then Tsimamanga went to the village. "Where does Papango Fito Loha dwell?" he asked.

And the people pointed the house of Papango Fito Loha that was in the river. So Tsimamanga made the river draw back. He blew the wind on it, "fo, fo, fo, fo," and the river drew back. And he went into the house of Papango Fito Loha. They had a talk.

"It's a good thing that you came," Papango Fito Loha said.

"Is that it?" Tsimamanga asked.

"Yes," the seven-headed thing said. And Papango Fito Loha asked Tsimamanga to come in, and when he was in the house, Papango Fito Loha took out an enormous pot. It asked ten of its servants to lift the pot onto the fire. Then Papango Fito Loha lifted Tsimamanga and dropped him into the enormous pot. The pot was usually used to carry water, or for a big share of meat for the sacrifice to the gods. But the seven-headed hawk meant to cook Tsimamanga. He turned him around and around and around. But while Tsimamanga was turning around, turning around in that huge pot, he took out his amulet, Valamangatsiritra, his golden amulet.

"Blow the wind on me three times," he commanded. And Valaman-gatsiritra blew, "fo, fo, fo." Tsimamanga was still turning around in the pot, but he lifted the huge pot all at once from the inside, and the pot broke into pieces. And he said, "Papango Fito Loha, we will fight to the death."

And they had a big fight. They fought and they fought and they fought. "This child is dangerous and powerful," Papango Fito Loha said, and fell to the ground. Tsimamanga was too powerful for Papango Fito Loha. And so Papango Fito Loha was defeated by Tsimamanga. It threw itself to the ground and died.

—as told by M. Soaraza
(Toliara)

෴෴෴෴෴

Just Head

Once upon a time, there were three brothers. The two eldest brothers were built perfectly but the youngest had just a head. That's why he was called Ylohasuau: Just Head. As the eldest and the middle brothers were already young men, they went in the woods and learned how to steal cows.

One day, the youngest brother asked to be with them, saying: "I'll go with you when you go to rob."

But they refused and said: "You'll get us caught by the men. No, we won't let you go over there." But finally they agreed, since they planned to leave him alone somewhere in the woods.

They went along the forest but when they saw a big river where fierce crocodiles were living, they pushed their brother in the water and left him. And they went on looking for cows and found a village where they stole many cows. When they came back home with a stable full of cows, everybody was happy. But when they turned their backs to celebrate the event, the cows were not there any more. They were disappointed and surprised. What is more, the cows had been sent back to their owners. Nobody realized that it was Just Head who drove away those cows. He was in the middle of the cows but nobody saw him. The owners were afraid to gather their cows again, since they thought it was a trap. But finally, he showed himself and tried to explain his fate and what happened and they believed him and he became respected and praised by the village people.

One day he told the owners of the cows: "Bring me ten of these big cows and arrange them in a line like an army and wrap them with rush straw and put them in a fire." So the people grilled the cows, and grilled and grilled. The smoke rose up to God. He was so dazzled by that smoke that he sent for his errand servant, Juorombe (Elephant Bird), to go down to the earth, and said: "Juorombe, go down and ask who dares to send this dazzling smoke up to me?" And Elephant Bird descended and asked this same question.

Just Head replied: "It's me, Just Head, who was not built by God."

The Elephant Bird, surprised, asked: "What?"

But Just Head just kept on repeating: "It's me, Just Head, who was not built by God."

So Elephant Bird went up to God and reported what Just Head had told him. God was so surprised that he ordered Elephant Bird to bring Just Head up to him. When he saw him, very poor, he ordered Elephant Bird to make him sit on the golden chair. But Just Head didn't want to be there, and he moved all the time, avoiding sitting there. Seeing his behavior, God summoned Elephant Bird again to put him into a big basin containing *rano mahuy* (strong water that holds the essence of life) to have a bath.

After he had had a bath, and a bath, and a bath, at last, God asked him: "How are you, little boy?"

Just Head replied: "I begin to have a throat."

"Keep on having a bath," said God. After a few moments, God asked him again. "How are you now?"

"I begin to have shoulders."

"Keep on having a bath."

And God asked him the same question after a few moments. "How are you now?"

"I have hands."

And he kept on having a bath until he had his full-length body. Then he was perfectly built and he came down to the earth.

When he got home, he showed himself to his family and said: "Father, I am here."

But the family did not believe him. And he said again: "I am Just Head though you did not want to keep me and left me alone in the woods." And his parents examined him and saw he was perfect and were happy. However, when his two brothers saw him, they became jealous and tried to challenge him. So they tried to reach God. They went up to him and asked him to make them perfect also.

And God said: "Elephant Bird, those young men want to be built perfectly because I didn't build them as they are supposed to be. Try to make them sit in the golden chairs." Elephant Bird did what God ordered him to do, and the two brothers went straight to the golden chairs and sat down. God, seeing their behavior, ordered Elephant Bird to put them in pudgy water (foul water that holds no life) and told them to have a bath. And they had a bath, they had a bath. After a few minutes, God asked them: "How are you, my boys?"

And they replied: "We begin to lose our hands."

"Keep on having a bath."

After a few moments, he asked them again. "How are you now?"

"We begin to lose our legs." And they kept on having a bath until they became two real dogs. They were sent back home and ordered to call their wives whose names were Bao and Vao. That's why Malagasy dogs, when they bark, say: "B——a- a- o- o" or "V- a- a- o- o." And from then to now, dogs cannot do without men, because they don't want to be separated from their wives, and they know they come from one source.

—as told by M. Soaraza
(Toliara)

ৡৢৡৢৡৢৡৢৡৢ

Babaky — Squash Boy

Once upon a time, there was a young man whose name was also Young Man, who was called Zatoro, and who was very rich and handsome. He had four wives and each of them had a part of his field. He had children from each of them but unfortunately the fourth wife delivered instead of a child, a squash. From that time, her "sisters" laughed at her all of the time and this child was treated as a little monster.

Since all of the four wives had a part of the field, they had to work their part. The three other wives always thought the fourth woman would never get her part plowed and would never get any crops because she did not have a child to help her as they all had. However, her husband realized that she was the only wife who had her part perfectly cultivated and plowed, and he was so amazed.

One day, since he had had enough of the other wives ceaselessly teasing and laughing at this wife, he told his mother, "Mother, on Friday I'd like to gather all the village people." His mother told Young Man to gather the people as he wished, and he did it.

The day came and the whole village was there including the other wives. When the ceremony began, Babaky, the Squash Child, showed himself and said to the people that he was not at all a squash but he was a real child like any other child. When they realized that he was truly a child, their joy burst out and praised him. The other wives were so surprised. And since that time the Squash Child and his mother were well treated by Young Man but the others were punished and left alone by their husband.

—as told by M. Soaraza
(Toliara)

CHAPTER III

TRAFFIC IN SALT COUNTRY

Antsirabe was a tourist town, complete with palm-lined avenues, cobblestone lanes, hot springs, and pleasant lakes reflecting the shadows of the Ankaratra massifs. The winds from the mountains wrapped the town in a year-round temperate climate, another reason for the popularity of its thermal springs. This scenic beauty was not lost on visitors. They came from great distances, commoners and royalty, not only from Madagascar, but from Europe as well. Over the years, their visits had influenced the architecture, the pattern of streets, indeed, the very rhythms of the town. In the 1950s, King Mohammed V of Morocco had spent his exile in Antsirabe, "taking the baths," I was told, and the town seemed set on living up to its claim to fame. "An enchanting town," Mme. Arianne said before I left Tana. "They are accustomed to foreigners, so you will make your way there with no problem." I did make my way there, but no journey was without its problems.

We had traveled from Tana by taxi-brousse—Tiana, Haingo, Serge, and I. I'd met Serge my first week in Madagascar when he came to interview for a position with me as translator. "I have much translation experience," he had said. Although I had not hired him, Serge had become somewhat of a fixture on the balcony of La Karthala, arriving some mornings when Tiana and I were still making plans for the day over our breakfast tea. He had not flown south with us to Toliara and Fort Dauphin, but when he'd heard we were going across the Highlands to Antsirabe, he'd Bogarted his way onto the trip. "I have some friends in that town," he'd said, dangling the promise of folklore contacts before my eager nose. That was how Serge came to be with us when we'd set off from Mme. Arianne's pension to find a car to take us to Antsirabe.

The schedules for cars-for-hire were rather loosely defined, but in order to find comfortable seats, we had to leave early. As soon as we reached the terminal, I saw why we needed the extra time. The terminal area was a sand lot, big enough for a carnival and easily covering three city blocks. It was filled with all manner of cars, busses, and minibuses waiting for passengers. Hundreds of people were milling about trying to find the best ride to this place or that, some of them with bundles and luggage carried on their heads, Malagasy style, but others, like us, toting suitcases. Although we'd planned a lengthy stay in Antsirabe, Serge carried only a briefcase. I was puzzled. We were going to be away for several days and he was traveling a bit light, but in the madness of loading and departures, I didn't have time to ask him about the rest of his luggage. Later, I would discover that his briefcase held only three items: a toothbrush, a tape of Whitney Houston, and an English dictionary. Looking back, I think it was just as well that I didn't have this bit of information as we scrambled for transportation to Antsirabe. Adding Serge to my list of concerns would have made our departure only more harrowing.

We trudged past several lines of minibuses that were already half full before Haingo recommended a taxi-brousse, one of the many cars-for-hire that was too small to be a bus, yet traveled too far to be a taxi. "We'll buy five seats in back," he said. "Less chance of being crammed in with too many other people." But I couldn't wrap my imagination around that many people in the rear seat of any sedan, so I refused to buy extra space in the taxi-brousse we hired. As it was, I already had to buy four seats because of Serge.

"Four seats will be plenty," I told Haingo, thinking that would take care of the whole car: three of us in the back seat, and one in the front seat along with the driver—according to my American concept, full capacity for any sedan. But I was traveling Malagasy style, and like the jitney taxis in the inner cities of America, the capacity of the car depended on the tolerance of the passengers. The driver began by putting Serge and Haingo in the front seat along with himself and another passenger. That totaled four in the front. Then he added another passenger to the back seat. By that time, the car was beginning to resemble a carnival ride, or one of those old phone booth gags that college fraternities try during hazing week. But I drew the line after yet another rider, including a school age child who sat on her mother's lap, climbed into the back with me and Tiana.

"Enough," I yelled, and held out more money. Haingo gave me an "I warned you" look as I tried to make a nest for my rear end in the ten inches of seat between me, Tiana, and the door. I was set to complain until I noticed a couple of minibuses pulling out of the lot, passengers all but hanging off the running boards. Serge turned around and smiled. "Comfortable?" he asked. I didn't answer. Later, when I realized it would take four hours to reach Antsirabe, I wished I'd bought two more seats.

The trip was four hours through rice fields and sparse forests where the black granite humps of the Ankaratra range studded the landscape like the backs of elephants, where the old ways reigned in villages so small that the name of the place was likely to be larger than the space it occupied, where mud grew right up to the door, and *fady* (taboos) governed everything from how to till the land to how *vitana* (fate) determined which corner of the house the husband should occupy.

Dikes, molded from red earth, made quilt patterns in the green rice fields, and as we bumped along on the rise and swell of rollercoaster roads, I began to wish that the same regularity had been applied to paving the macadam. A four-hour ride on any Madagascar road was enough to make a person a believer in air travel. Not that Madagascar had a monopoly on bad roads; the same narrow, rutted, poorly planned trails that pass for roads could be found in eastern Europe, South America, and Africa. They were roads without speed limits and no easement space on the shoulders. On those roads, drivers also zipped past beater cars driving in tandem, passed on the blind side of uphill grades, or lingered almost a fraction of a second too long in the oncoming lane as they raced to overtake slow moving trucks. And drivers on those other roads also barreled around curves in aging cars that almost managed to attain warp speed, despite bad pistons and rings that left a belch of black smoke inside an umbrella of dust, albeit dust that was not as colorful as Madagascar's red soil.

Our driver proceeded with the absolute conviction that he'd overtake the next bus, the next car clouded in its own thick exhaust. I tried to settle into his stick shift pattern of drive, brake, swerve, brake, accelerate — not a rhythm but an off rhythm, like the jerky tune of a new musician trying to figure out jazz improvisations. The snores of those who could relax provided the downbeat. Serge's head nodded in tune to the jolt of ruts in the road, and the child in her mother's lap woke up and groaned each time we passed through a town. But as the driver swerved into the oncoming lane, zigged when he should have zagged, or failed to accelerate when speed was our only salvation, the beauty of the landscape was lost inside the pocket of anxiety I carried with me. We covered miles of highway that twisted upon itself past zebu tracks and two-story houses staring at the road through unshuttered windows. I told myself that it was no worse than other roads I'd traveled. The only difference was that with the crush of passengers crammed into the taxi-brousse, I was numb from the waist down when we reached Antsirabe.

In English, the word *Antsirabe* translates into "place of much salt," but what I remember was a place of many vehicles: some fast, some slow, some stuttering along at a pace that seemed more fitting to the nineteenth century that had spawned the town than the twentieth century it was struggling with. On my first afternoon in Antsirabe, I sat at an intersection and watched a parade of cars, buses, horses, bicycles, zebu-drawn carts, the rickshaw-like pousse-pousse, even a boat that was longer than the truck hauling it — a parade that moved in both directions in an endless stream.

There was something grand about that wash of traffic, something elegant in the way these conveyances moved across the wide-lane boulevard, clearing the shadows of trees long enough to allow dapples of sunlight to decorate the fringed top of a pousse-pousse, the brown skin of a barefoot boy riding a chestnut mare that pranced like a show horse, the straw hat of a man leading a humpbacked bullock by a thick rope of woven raffia, and of course, the eternal scene in Madagascar: a woman, market-bound from some outlying village, walking with regal elegance, a basket on her head and a lamba wrapped around her hips.

It was the kind of colorful scene that filled nostalgic travel posters for the colonial avenues of old Singapore or the French Quarter in New Orleans. Usually, all I needed was a small reminder to feed my passion to join the crowd heading toward some poster perfect spot. But that afternoon, I was already a part of some imaginary poster, and that afternoon, I was road-weary.

At first, I was paying more attention to my own comfort than to the scene around me, but slowly I began to take notice. Haingo had arranged for pousse-pousse transportation after we'd checked into the Villa Nirina, the pension that would be our home while we were in Antsirabe. Because there were four of us—Serge again—we'd hired two of the foot-powered cabs. Some pousse-pousse owners leaned toward elaborate decorations, but the one I was in was a rather plain affair by Antsirabe standards: a worn, rust red leather seat and a frayed retractable canopy, the rainflap undecorated, the frame painted robin's egg blue. All I saw was the breathing room, the space to lean back and cross my legs without folding in on myself like a piece of origami.

I preferred to wait while Tiana led Haingo and Serge through the paperwork trail of local departments of culture and antiquity. I watched them walk into the office, then settled back to the luxury of occupying a whole seat by myself. The drivers were resting on the curb, one sprawled out flat on the grass and the other staring off into the distance. I followed his gaze. That's when I noticed the intersection—the traffic flowing steadily but quietly. No jangle of motorcycles and sirens. No blasts of horns or squeal of tires. Just a steady flow, like water over rocks, over the smooth path of a clear stream. I aimed my camera, thinking I needed to wait for just the right moment, that second when the traffic, like planets in conjunction, showed me both the past and the present sharing the same horizon. But there was no need to wait. The traffic continued, unabated — horses, cars, carriages, bicycles, and pousse-pousse runners moving at a steady clip.

When we started up again, I watched the stride of the pousse-pousse driver. He was a light brown-skinned man with angular, handsome features—a shaved head, a thin mustache, and gaunt cheeks that, I suspected, made him look older than he was. Years of work as a pousse-pousse runner had toughened his body. He was sinewy and long, and he ran with the same loping stride that Jesse Owens had had in film clips I'd seen of the 1936 Olympics in Munich. The other pousse-pousse driver, the one carrying Haingo and Serge as passengers, had a more stocky build, but what he lacked in the length of his stride, he made up for with speed. Our driver always let him set the pace of the trip.

"They will share the fare," Tiana said. "They have to earn enough to buy their carriages."

"They'd make great runners," I said. Then I stopped myself. That thought was far too Western. What made me presume that the work of the pousse-pousse driver was different from that of a coal miner or a steelworker? What I saw as sports competition was economic survival. Still, that did not keep me from admiring the stamina of the men who pulled the carriages.

Whenever we had to stop, I could tell that the drivers were winded. When Haingo motioned for Tiana to get out of the carriage, I asked him if we shouldn't share a bottle of mineral water with the drivers. I'd bought half a dozen, and with Serge and the drivers, there was just enough to go around. The air was thin and dry, the water sweet tasting, and with our view of the hills on the horizon, I thought, once again, how picture perfect the landscape seemed.

No matter where we went, I felt as if we were straddling some invisible line, one side that would let Antsirabe rush into modern life, and one that held it in the throes of some other era. On wide streets bordered by palm trees, Swiss chalets hid behind English flower gardens, and French country houses boasted thick hedges of bougainvillea. Along narrow streets, I was as likely to find young Malagasy boys playing the Italian game of boccie ball as I was to see old men sitting curbside, caught up in an intense game of *fanorona*. There were wide avenues that were far too busy to accommodate boccie or *fanorona*. On the Avenue des Thermes, the grand Hotel des Thermes was an echo of the elegant hotels of Europe; it ruled the north shore of Lake Ranomafana like some dinosaur caught forever in the mouth of the thermal springs. Its architecture danced between French and Moroccan, all curlicues and symmetry rendered in dark wood and shadowed by elaborate gardens. Below it, Lake Ranomafana glistened. The weeping willows ringing its shores trailed their fronds across the water like lace. The lake beckoned us to stop. I waved to the pousse-pousse carrying Haingo and Serge.

"We have an appointment to see a professor of literature who lives on the other side of town," Tiana said. "And Haingo knows about this woman who tells stories to children."

"But the lake," I said. "It is so beautiful." The lake winked in agreement.

"There is a legend that a princess drowned in this lake," Haingo said. "That is why it is *fady* to wash in this water."

"And some say they can still see her swimming to the middle of the lake," Serge added.

"But if she could swim, why did she drown?" I asked.

"It is just a story," Tiana said.

"That's what we're after," I laughed, and signaled to move on.

At the conjunction of the Avenue de l'Indépendance and the Avenue de M. Foch, we turned toward Asabotsy market, where the line between the present and the past seemed to fade. While hotels like Thermes, Diamant, and Truchet echoed their European designs, the market had remained nearly unsullied by the colonial era of Madagascar. It carried its ties to the country's past with the same casual ease that rural women carried water jugs and baskets on their heads. It was the center of commerce for a dozen tiny villages near Antsirabe. People came to the market by truck, by bus, by horse, by bike—and of course, by pousse-pousse.

As soon as we neared the market, our pousse-pousse drivers were forced to slow from a loping run and jockey for position in the flow of traffic. For a while, we were caught in an erratic conga line, traffic weaving like a dragon's tail of dancers off to find some endless New Year's celebration. Women passed us carrying fowl by their feet. Heads down, the birds had fallen into a quiet stupor. "Tonight's supper," Tiana said. At one corner, I saw yards of embroidered linen billowing like sails. At another, root medicines and spices rested side by side in cardboard boxes, their colors as vivid as a painter's palette. I caught a whiff of fresh peppers careening off the smells of ground mustard and cumin, a trace of camphor fingering the air. But all of it was tempered by the aroma of fresh twigs of vanilla, bouquets of mint, and newly tanned leather hanging from wires above the vendors' stalls.

I suppose I would have been willing to sit back and enjoy the pousse-pousse ride if I hadn't already been on the road from Tana since early morning, but when I noticed that we'd traveled down the same street three times, my body simply refused to find a comfortable spot on that seat. "Aren't we supposed to be looking for the woman who tells children's stories?" I asked Tiana. "Mme. Rajaonah. Didn't the Haingo say she lives near the market?"

"No," Tiana said. "She lives on the other side of town. We are going to a house where Serge knows some people. It is near the park."

Serge, I thought. Serge of the mysterious briefcase. The idea of Serge as our navigator made me a little uneasy for reasons I couldn't quite pinpoint. My conversations with Serge always seemed to take odd turns where I ended up talking about some subject without knowing how I'd gotten there. Maybe this ride was going the same route as Serge's conversations. "The park is east of the lake," I said to Tiana, "and we are still circling the market."

She shrugged. "I think Serge is lost," she said.

"So what else is new?" I said. "Well, if he's got a map in that briefcase, I hope he pulls it out now." I was beginning to feel a little testy. Even in a picture perfect world, I couldn't imagine myself trapped forever in a crazy traffic pattern. Then Serge redeemed himself—for the moment—and we turned away from the market and crossed Avenue de l'Indépendance. In a quagmire of streets north of the market, we stopped.

"We have to walk from here," Serge beckoned.

"Serge, we've been riding around for hours," I said.

He turned. "Madame, if I should ever traffic you . . ."

"Traffic," I said. "That's it! It's the traffic. I've had it with the traffic!"

For a second, Serge looked puzzled, then he said, "This way," and started walking down a narrow street.

I fell into step behind him. "What does he mean by traffic me?" I asked Tiana.

"I don't know," she said. "It is an English phrase."

"Not any phrase I've heard," I told her. I puzzled over what was obviously Serge's personal slant on English translation, but for the second time that day, I didn't have a chance to ask him to explain.

We walked toward a clutch of buildings down a street so narrow not even the pousse-pousse drivers could have worked their way to the door. There was no mistaking the difference between the affluence of the neighborhood around the Hotel Thermes, and the streets in this part of town. This was the section of working class poor in a tourist town—not poor by village standards in places where crops had failed and folks lived in shanties, or as poor as those who came daily to Antananarivo, the beggars who haunted the square near the Zoma market—but a part of town with dirt roads and one-story houses cocooned in a maze of kitty-cornered streets. This was more village than town, like hamlets in Germany, Hungary, or Yugoslavia, or mining towns in Appalachia, and like those places, the inside of the houses mirrored the outside.

Outside, the sky was overcast in rainy season gray, and when I stepped inside, I didn't find much change in the light: a square, dimly lit room, with doors and windows on the west wall, in accordance with Malagasy philosophy in which the design of the house reflected time and destiny. Cardboard boxes, stacked beside the entryway, seemed to absorb more light. There were boxes in the main room too, stashed in the corner as if the owners were still unpacking. The main room—the front room, as my grandmother would have called it—was full of heavy brocaded furniture, festooned with lace doilies that soaked up what little illumination the single overhead bulb offered. The room was made darker by the way the lace window curtains diffused the light. It was very warm, a small fire grate with burning coals heating the air. Cooking smells wafted in from somewhere in back of the house. A stew, I thought. Too pungent for beef. Goat, perhaps. The smell was so strong, I could almost taste it. Everything was close in the room, but there was a cheeriness about it, a comfortable lived-in feeling that I had not seen in some of the homes in Tana, those that were furnished with shipments directly from France. Still, the French influence could not be missed in the style of the sagging Louis XIV sofa where we sat in that flat in Antsirabe. But with seven people crowded into the small room, talk did not center on the preference for French designs. In fact, there was not much talk at all at first.

   Introductions were made. "Mes amies," Serge told me, "M. William et s'épouse. M. Henri et s'épouse." Tiana whispered that they were brothers. The men and their wives nodded. They gave me the seat of honor, mid-sofa. I was the visitor, the American. We all said, "*Akory e! Akory e!*"

Both couples were relatively young, in their late thirties, I imagined. They were of medium height, with the broad features and dark brown complexion of the Betsileo people. Henri's eyes were light brown—"cat eyes" my family called them. Several children, looking like mirror images of their parents, came and went, melting in and out of the room like shadows until they were sent to play. Then we just sat, smiling.

"Do they know why we're here?" I asked Tiana.

"Maybe," she said. "If Serge tells them."

Serge again. With Serge in charge, it was as if we'd simply stumbled into someone's house, and they had been far too polite to ask us to leave. I wondered why they were home in the first place. It was midday, and the men were dressed in their work clothes: short-sleeved shirts and pants, a hat to shield them from the sun. "They work in the market," Serge had said, but their house was some distance away from the market. I wondered what Serge had told them, what slight bend of translation had enticed them to meet with us. Then I understood. Having brought us this far, Serge wasn't sure of the next step. So much for "I have much translation experience," I thought. I began to make small talk. The room was a collection of country and family: small objects, ceramic and wood engraved with symbols of Madagascar, and photos everywhere. I admired the lace on the back of the sofa, and the piece framing the doorway.

"Hand embroidered?" I asked. Tiana translated. Our hosts nodded. The woman of the house grinned. "It is beautiful," I said in French. "*Tsara tarehy ity*," Tiana repeated in Malagasy. Serge nodded and nodded. "*Tsara tarehy ity. Tsara tarehy ity.*"

It wasn't much of a beginning. I spoke one language. Tiana and Haingo translated, and Serge sounded like he was babbling, but it worked. We drank sweet cups of coffee and looked at pictures of sons and daughters who had moved to Tana or England or France. Most were sepia prints that were fading into the light of the past. Children and grandchildren. A young married couple, the woman beautiful, the man handsome. "Henri?" I asked, noting the resemblance. Haingo asked about the picture of a young man in uniform, a nephew who had been decorated by the French in World War II, then died in Madagascar in the uprising against the French a scant two years later. They asked about my life in New York, and I tried to describe the Pacific Northwest. "The opposite coast," I said. "Rain, like here but without the palm trees." It was a little disconcerting to have three translators, especially with Serge breaking in now and then like a nervous teenager on a first date. I think everyone was happy when I finally brought out the tape recorder. The men took over, both M. Henri and M. William offering a story that they told almost as one. Their wives laughed at their hesitations. They seemed to be creating the story, yet keeping to the theme—nudging each other with the memory of details and laughing at their mistakes, each embellishing until the story, like the changing patterns of light and shadow, took on its own nuance.

"It is the story of three brothers," Tiana whispered. And I began to hear the repetition of events, the pattern of the story: the brothers, the three attempts at success, the warnings to avoid pitfalls. Henri and William added gestures, enriching the trials and the obstacles to be overcome. It was a universal story of heroism, of good over evil, of duty and honor.

"*Angano*," Serge said. "*Angano*."

ℓℓℓℓℓ

The Three Brothers

Once upon a time, there were three brothers who were orphans and their relatives did not want to look after them. (Orphans whose family despised them.) One day, the eldest said to his brothers: "We are so poor, so let me go and look for what will keep us alive."

"But what about both of us? Will you leave us lonely?"

"I know, but I have to leave you," the eldest said, "and before leaving,

I'm going to plant a banana tree in the west part of our village, and when it is dead, I'll be dead. But if it grows up, I'll be alive and it will bring us luck and fortune."

The two brothers said, "Well, let us prepare some food for your long journey."

"No, let me go now," and they said goodbye and he left. He went away, away, away and when the night fell, he was in the middle of the woods. He was terrified and said to himself, "Where can I go this night? There's not any shelter here, and animals are very fierce. Oh my god, please help me."

Suddenly, he found a small hut, but he wondered if it was not an enemy's shelter. At last, he decided to come near it and knock on the door. An old man answered:

"Who's that?"

"A visitor coming from a distant region and come to look for work."

"Come in, come in, my little boy. You can sleep in my hut."

But the eldest hesitated and said: "No grandfather, let me stay outside."

"Do come in, because I have something to tell you."

And he came in.

"Now, let me get something to eat for you," said the old man.

The old man cooked him some food, and after it was served, he had a good meal. After having finished it, he said, "Please grandfather, let me sleep because I feel so tired and so sleepy. Can I sleep now?"

"No, I cannot let you sleep. I have something to show you."

"What is it, grandfather?"

"Do you know, I have a cat who is able to hold a lantern?"

"I cannot believe it. You're lying. A cat can never hold a light."

"You can't?" said the old man. "If you don't trust me, what is the bet? If my cat can't hold the light, you kill me. If it can hold the lantern, I'll kill you. So if I'm lying, you'll kill me, but if it is true, I'll kill you."

Then he called the cat and said, "Take this candle." The cat obeyed and held it until dawn. At which time, the old man killed the eldest brother. When the young man was dead, he put him into a barrel where there were other corpses.

In the meantime, in the village, the banana tree was dead and both of the younger brothers knew their brother was also dead.

So the middle brother decided and said to the youngest, "Our brother is dead. I have to leave you and look for his corpse. And for a job somewhere to make life better."

But the youngest said, "Where shall I go without both of you? Who is going to take care of our small possessions? If ever you die somewhere else, what shall I do?"

"No, be hopeful. But I have to leave you. Don't worry, I'll find our elder brother."

And he planted another banana tree. When the night fell, he was in the woods. He was terrified and said, "Where am I now? There's nothing here. Oh God, help me." Some time later, he found a small hut and decided to knock on the door.

The old man asked, "Who is that?"

"A poor orphan with no one to look after him, scorned by our relatives, and has come to earn his living. My house is very far from here and I can't go back."

"Come in little boy and let me get something for you to eat. You must be very hungry."

"No grandfather, I prefer sleeping because I am very tired."

"No, you have to take some dinner." He cooked sweet potatoes for him. The young boy ate his food and asked the old man for a place to sleep near the oven because he was very cold.

"No, I can't let you sleep, because I have something to show you."

"What's that, grandfather?"

"Do you know I have a cat who is able to hold a candle?"

"You tell me a lie, grandfather. It is impossible."

"If you don't believe me, what's the bet? So if I lie, kill me but if it is true, I'll kill you."

"Oh no, how can I kill you, for you are a respectful parent. It's impossible for me."

The old man said, "It doesn't matter. The cat always does this by habit until dawn." And then he called the cat again and made it hold the candle. And it lasted until dawn. And he killed the young man. When he died, the second banana tree also died.

When the youngest knew that his brother was dead, he was so sad and decided to look for his brothers. "How can I live like this?" he said. "I am alone. No father, no mother, no brother. I am nothing." He left the village and went away, away, away. At last, when the night fell, he reached the middle of the woods and found the small hut. He knocked on the door and the old man asked, "Who's that?"

"A visitor from the other side of the village who comes to look for work. My elder and younger brother left to look for work and I don't know where they are now. That's why I am here. To look for them."

"Come in, come in, little boy."

The youngest brother entered and the old man told him to have a seat because he was going to prepare a meal for him. When leaving the youngest brother, he said in a low voice, "It will be a good meal again."

But the boy heard that and realized that it was the old man who had killed his brothers. When the old man came back, the youngest brother ate and finally asked the old man if he could sleep. But the old man said, "I can't let you sleep right now."

"But I am so tired, grandfather."

"No, I still have something to show you."

"What is that, grandfather?"

"It is a cat who can hold a candle."

"It is a lie. I have never seen a cat holding a candle in my life."

"But what is the bet? So if I am a liar, you'll kill me but if it is the truth, I'll kill you."

"Yes, I agree but let me first go out for a few moments, because I have something wrong in my stomach."

"Go outside," the old man said.

When he was out, he looked for small mice and found them. He hid them in his pockets and came in again. When the old man saw him, he called the cat and said, "My cat, my dear cat, take this candle."

The cat took the candle and held it. However, after a few hours, the youngest brother got one of the mice out. When the cat saw the mouse, it dropped the candle and fell upon the mouse. The boy said to the old man, "You see, you are a liar."

The old man was furious and said to the cat, "You nasty cat. Take this candle."

The cat came and held it again. But after a few moments, the boy got his mouse out again and the cat ran after it but it was already dawn. The old man failed and should have been killed by the boy. But as he was terribly afraid, he said to the boy, "I beg your forgiveness. Don't kill me. I've already killed many people."

"So you have also killed my brothers? If you don't make them come to life again, I'll kill you."

The old man went out and took a strange stick of wood and beat the water in the barrel with it. Everyone in the barrel came to life again and the two brothers were among them. Afterwards, when the youngest was ready to kill the old man, one of the brothers said, "Don't kill him because he will be cursed all his life by what he has done."

—as told by M. Henri and M. William
(Antsirabe)

When we left the house of M. Henri and M. William and returned to the Villa Nirina, it was nearly dark. As we listened to the tape, Serge said, "This *angano* I have heard many times when I was a boy."

"Then you won't have any trouble helping Tiana and Haingo transcribe it," I said to him.

"I am prepared," he said, and pulled a dictionary from his briefcase.

That's when I discovered the contents of the case he'd hung onto so tightly during our trip. That dog-eared dictionary and a single audio-tape, without a player. The case, which had looked so official, was reduced to a sack, not enough to see him through a class, much less a weekend of field research.

"Serge, do you always take your dictionary with you?" I asked, diplomatically ignoring the Whitney Houston tape.

"It's not much of a dictionary," Haingo said, thumbing through the book.

As I reached for the book, Serge pleaded, "Madame, if I should ever traffic you, please to let me know."

I waved that ratty dictionary under his nose. "Serge, is this where you got that traffic stuff? If so, put it back. Traffic is not what people do." I paused. "At least, not legally," I added. "Traffic is what cars do. You know, like the car you arranged for tomorrow." He looked puzzled. "Serge, you did arrange a car for tomorrow, didn't you?"

"A car? Yes, madame. A car. If I should ever . . ."

I held up my hand. "Don't say it, Serge. Please, don't say it."

Haingo had planned for us to meet with a storyteller the next day in Betafo, a village about fourteen miles from Antsirabe. Serge had been sent to hire a car to take us there. What kind of trafficking could Serge imagine? I asked myself. I hoped his translation from English to Malagasy was clearer than his translation from Malagasy to English. I looked him in the eyes.

"Tell me," I said. "Tell me that you have found a car for us."

"Madame, if I should ever . . . ," he began.

I handed back his dictionary and gave my fate to the goddess of all researchers.

Serge had found a car for us, but as we rumbled along on the road between Antsirabe and Betafo, I gained a growing appreciation for the taxi-brousse that had carried us from Tana. True, that driver had studied with Evel Knievel or Parnelli Jones, but for all of his lurching and heart-stopping curves, the taxi-brousse had run smoothly. His was a gazelle compared to the car Serge had hired. Serge's car was a bullock. It bucked, wheezed, and protested on the level sections of road. On the uphill, and that included even the slightest incline, it rebelled by leaking smoke through the glove compartment — or rather, the space where a glove compartment had been. To reduce the smoke, the driver simply cut the engine. That left us moving backward more than forward, sometimes coming to a halt in the middle of the road before the engine had cooled enough to allow us to resume speed.

Fortunately, the road was not as heavily traveled as the Tana highway. Zebu-drawn carts and ancient buses weaved past us, but it was still unnerving to sit in the middle of the road while people on foot passed us. They peered at us through the windows and smiled sympathetically. We sat there coughing and fanning away smoke. "Let's get moving," I said. Speed was not in the vocabulary of that engine. Movement was more like a fast idle that didn't require braking, which was a good thing because the brakes were in worse shape than the clutch, a peculiar mechanism that squawled its discontent all the way to Betafo.

Serge made an effort to put me at ease. "Some say Betafo is the oldest village in the Highlands," he announced.

"Will it still be there when we arrive?" I asked.

"It's only a few miles away," Haingo said.

"Tell the car," I muttered.

Serge looked heartbroken. I turned to the window.

The architecture of Antsirabe had been left behind, and now we were among the narrow, two-story adobe houses of village design. Tile roofs bore witness to the heavy rains that swept across the region. Fields of corn slid by the window. We were moving so slowly, I could have counted the number of stalks in any given row. Patches of agave plants broke the symmetry from time to time. "Those are for making sisal," Tiana said. The car coughed in agreement. In the distance, the Ankaratra range was cloaked in a mist that turned the hills into purple silhouettes of themselves. A hint of cool breezes from the Ankaratra brushed against the

Hillside houses bathed in morning sunlight, Antananarivo

Diviner in the sacred circle, Ambohimanga (Blue Mountain)

(*opposite*) Manindry Dance Troupe performing lake spirit dance, Toliara

(*top*) Storyteller, M. Soaraza, Toliara

(*bottom*) Pousse-pousse driver, Antsirabe

(*top*) Papermaker adding flowers to bark pulp, Fianarantsoa

(*bottom*) Musicians playing *jejy voatavo* outside Chez Papillon, Fianarantsoa

(*opposite*) Hiragasy
orator in red frock
coat places his hat
on the drum before
addressing the
ancestors, Antananarivo

(*right*) Hiragasy
singer at ceremony
in Antananarivo

(*bottom*)
Hiragasy singers giving
impromptu performance,
Ambondrona

Preparing funeral feast, Ambondrona

Funeral elders and mourners, Ambondrona

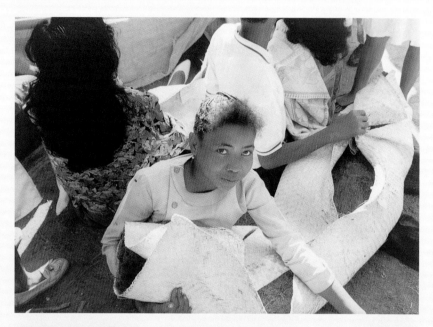

(*top*) Famadihana, young girl holding her ancestor, near Antananarivo

(*bottom*) Famadihana placing the ancestors in the tomb, near Antananarivo

(*top*) Sacred tree with ribbons and offerings for the ancestors, Lake Mangatsa

(*bottom*) Young storyteller, Efraim Romaine (in red shirt), Ambalatoratasy

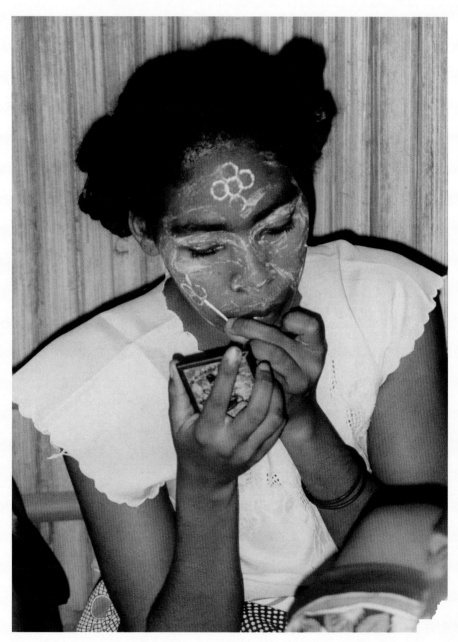

Applying Mangary paste, Boina settlement, Mahajanga

clusters of sisal plants, their tall, center stalks crowned with a single bloom that was as golden as Kansas wheat. We may not have had the best transport, but the sky was cloudless and the winds were calm. Serge's car aside, it was a breathtaking view.

When we arrived in Betafo, Mme. Victoria, the storyteller we were seeking, was working in the fields. Someone went to fetch her and we were told to return in a couple of hours in order to give her a chance to come in from the fields and change out of her work clothes. That gave us time to explore. Serge pointed out landmarks. There was the cattle market in the center of town where horses and ridge-backed zebus waited to be sold. "This place is famous for its horses," Haingo said. "And the churches," Serge added. On the other side of the square, an impressively large Catholic church looked more like it belonged in Antsirabe than in the market village of Betafo. In fact, there were churches and monuments throughout the town; the former left by missionaries and the latter by the revolution. Like many Malagasy towns, Betafo held impressive stone markers dedicated to revolutionary heroes. "A great warrior," Serge said as he pointed to one that dated back to King Radama I. One warrior's tomb was located at the top of a steep hill. From there, the lakes surrounding Betafo were visible.

"In this town, there are some stories about the Vazima, the first people of Madagascar," Tiana said. "Many of those stories happen near the water."

I looked around. Water, water everywhere: Lake Anosy, Antafofo Falls, and Tatamarina Lake. I caught sight of a lake far off in the distance. "Is that Lake Tritriva?" I asked, knowing we were scheduled to go there after we left Betafo.

"Maybe," Tiana said, "but I don't think so. There are many lakes near Betafo."

"And all of them have stories," Haingo said.

"I'm beginning to notice that," I told him.

"But the stories in Betafo are different," Serge said.

"You wouldn't traffic me, would you?" I teased.

He blinked, then gave me a boyish grin.

We took a route away from town in order to visit the old thermal baths in the crook of a narrow road outside of Betafo. The car took us halfway up the hill, then balked at climbing any higher. We walked the rest of the way. It was a natural spring. In a cluster of bathhouses, like the Roman baths I'd seen at Pompeii and Ephesus, stone benches surrounded cistern pits where hot mineral springs seeped into a basin.

"Do people still come up here?" I asked.

"Sometimes on holiday," Haingo said.

"I have been here," Serge said. I raised an eyebrow. "Yes, many times," he said. "In the spring, the water is fresh."

"It's the same water," Haingo said, "but in the spring, there is more of it. So many people come here in the spring."

"Do you?" I asked.

"When he has a girlfriend," Tiana laughed.

The bathhouses were lined up at the rim of the hill where the runoff of the mineral springs ended. When we walked around the corner, we saw two women beating agave leaves against smooth black rocks to soften them for the sisal fiber that they would later weave into baskets, floor mats, and burial shrouds. The long, tough leaves slapped against the rocks like wet laundry.

"The hot water helps soften the plant," Tiana said.

The work seemed tedious and repetitive, but the women never stopped to look up as we passed them and headed back down the hill.

I think both the driver and car were grateful that the trip back to town was downhill. We coasted most of the way, and the driver looked relieved when I told him we'd find our own way back. I didn't relish hiring another car, but the thought of riding inside the belly of that monster didn't seem a reasonable option.

"Tell him to fix that jalopy," I told Serge. "It's like riding downwind of a fire."

Serge nodded yes and yes, but when we were leaving Betafo, I thought

Storyteller, Mme. Victoria (*right*) with her sister, in Betafo

I saw the driver, another passenger seated in the back, creeping down the road toward to Antsirabe. But I could barely make out his face for the smoke that clouded the inside.

Good fortune was with me for the rest of the day. Mme. Victoria, the first woman storyteller I met, made us feel at home. We gathered in the main room with her, her sister, and a neighbor—a cousin, I was told, a young man who seemed to be there more because Haingo and Serge were strange men entering the house. The neighbor took the chair in that corner of the house reserved for men in accordance with Betsileo tradition. The house was not much different from the house of M. Henri and M. William that we'd visited in Antsirabe—small and sparsely furnished with crocheted doilies, lace curtains, photos of relatives, and mementos of Madagascar carved in stone and wood scattered throughout the room.

Like her sister, Mme. Victoria was dressed in the manner of a country woman: sandals, a loose fitting blouse and skirt, her head wrapped in a scarf. She was an older woman—"a grandmother," she said—her deep-set eyes full of humor and wisdom. Hers was a face burnished by sun and wind and the caprice of weather. The strength in her hands came from being a farmer's wife, but she kept to the old skills of embroidery as well.

"She says she used to sew for herself," Tiana translated, "but now she has many grandchildren and no time to make curtains."

A breeze picked up the gossamer lace of the curtains and they fluttered like a bride's veil. I asked Tiana to tell her how beautiful they were, the stitches invisible to my untrained eye. I couldn't imagine, in the course of my life, spending that much time handstitching a single item. When she offered me a cup of tea, she apologized for the roughness of her hands, but I saw no roughness, only gentility, a demeanor I had seen in both country and urban women in Madagascar. There was a gracefulness about her, her voice melodic, often not rising much above a whisper.

When I was in Tana, one of the students who had come to La Karthala to discuss African American music and literature had asked me how she might learn "to sing with her whole body." She was talking about the recordings she'd heard of black gospel singers. "In this country, even at *hiragasy*, the songs are not loud. But in America, one singer can make music fill the room."

I tried to explain how, in black churches, the choir sings so that God would hear. "At least, that is how I understand it," I said. "I guess it is a religious custom, just as it is a custom for your people to sing quietly to the ancestors who are never far away."

I wasn't sure that was the answer she wanted to hear, or for that matter that it was any answer at all, but I understood what she was trying to say. I had seen it, especially among the storytellers and singers, a kind of hush as if they were straining to hear the next line of the story or song, as if they were listening for the first time to words that had been told and retold.

When Mme. Victoria began to tell her stories, the room fell quiet. She told us tales of love and courage, the folly of youth and the wisdom of age. They were stories of magic, of shapechangers, of the very spirit of the earth. "In Betafo," Tiana told me, "they say that the people of the forest, the first people of this place, live as the spirits of the trees." It was easy to believe. As Mme. Victoria's stories unfolded, they seemed to take on a life of their own, words dancing in the air as the lace curtains billowed in the breeze. Even Serge, who seemed more comfortable in Betafo than he had been in Antsirabe, listened carefully. I watched him, the briefcase placed on the floor beside him, almost forgotten, and I wondered along what road into his childhood had the story taken him. We were all caught up in the act of storytelling, Mme. Victoria carrying each of us along some familiar path where home and families dwelled.

> *Ankanga Ankora maneno lohataona; ka ny tenako be no aty, fa ny saiko any Ankaratra ihany.*
> In the spring when I am here, my body
>   goes about like a mindless guinea fowl
>   making loud clucking noises, but my
>   mind goes far away to beautiful
> Ankaratra.

ഗ്ഗ്ഗ്ഗ്ഗ്

Two Girls and the Old Woman

Once upon a time, an old woman who couldn't have any children lived alone. One day, two sisters, Pelezy and her obedient younger sister, who were orphans and poor, went by the old woman's hut. The old woman saw them and asked, "Where are you going, my little daughters?"

They answered, "We are going to the East, Grandmother."

"Don't go there. You know Itrionobe, the monster, lives there."

"Don't worry, Grandmother. We'll never let Itrionobe, that trifling thing, capture us."

And they felt in their pockets for the maize and rice grains they had brought with them. The old woman warned them a second time, but they went on their way.

When they had walked a little farther, Itrionobe saw them and exclaimed, "*Maimbo Olombelona*." (I smell someone's odor.) When the two sisters saw the monster had followed them, they threw the maize and rice in the way of the monster and went running.

The monster, seeing that, thought, Those silly girls! Why do they throw away such a good meal? At the same time, he gathered all of the grains. Then he went on pursuing the girls. He ran like the wind. The little girls saw him, and again began to throw the grains.

Itrionobe thought those girls were stupid and said to himself, This good meal should not be thrown away. Again he gathered the grain and kept on running like the wind.

As he came closer to the girls, they grew very afraid and began to lose their courage. However, one of them had an idea, and said, "If my father or my mother were noble, they would make us become two orange trees."

And they became two beautiful orange trees. When Itrionobe, the monster, came near the trees and saw them, he was tempted to gather some of the fruit. But the trees were so thorny, he could not do anything, so he went on running to catch up with the little girls, since he did not know that those two orange trees were the girls he had been chasing.

After the monster ran away, away, away into the East, the little girls went back to the old woman. As soon as she saw them at a distance, she welcomed them with a song:

Oh! Pelezy Oh! Pelezy
Here are your pieces of chicken
Here are your balls of rice

And the girls replied:

Oh! our grandmother Oh! our grandmother
We are coming, we are coming
We are your daughters, coming very soon to your hut

And the old woman said, "Come in, my little girls. I am waiting for
you. I have already prepared some food."
And so, the little girls became her daughters. They lived together
and they inherited her.

—as told by Mme. Victoria
(Betafo)

જી જી જી જી જી

Rafaravavy and Randrianoro

Once upon a time, a nobleman had three children. His son called himself Randrianoro and his daughters were Ranakandriana, child of a
noble, and Rataluola, the youngest. Their parents were looking for a wife
for their son, but he refused any woman they suggested. Soon they had
enough of his refusals and told him to look himself for his future wife.

One day, while he was arranging something in his room, someone
knocked at the door and told Randrianoro that there were three beautiful girls he'd never seen playing in the sand at the edge of the lake. He
was amazed by their beauty and told the man he wanted to take one of
them as a wife. But the man advised him to take care by saying, "Since
they look like mermaids, it will be difficult for you to capture them if
you don't see a diviner."

Randrianoro asked him, "Who's this diviner I have to see?"

The man answered, "Ranakambo is the best one."

And so the boy went to see Ranakambo, the diviner, who ordered him to plant three beautiful orange trees in the sand to capture, he said, the first one who comes to gather some fruit there.

However, the three sisters were very careful and did not touch any of the trees. They warned each other, "Don't touch these trees. They are just traps."

So Randrianoro and the diviner failed. But Randrianoro again came to consult the diviner, and this time he was told, "Build a blue lake in the middle of the river and capture the one who comes playing there." But the eldest sister was clever enough and ordered her two sisters to be careful. "Do not play in this lake. It is nothing but a trap." And they did not play around the river.

Realizing his failure again, Randrianoro came back to the diviner, who advised him to become an ant so that he would not be recognized by the three girls.

He became an ant and stuck himself to the youngest sister, then quickly changed himself to a man again, telling her his wish to have her as a wife. But she answered, "I am not the wife who deserves you, my master, since we don't share the same way of living. I am not living on the earth. I am living in the heavens where my father also lives. When he knows you will want me to be your wife and when his mouth opens to tell you something, the thunder will burst and you will be terrified. Also, I don't drink alcohol. If you drink it, I will die. That's why we can't become husband and wife."

But Randrianoro replied, "I love you too much, so I will be careful about your taboos." And he took the girl to his family's house. His parents were so happy welcoming Rafaravavy, the youngest sister of the heavens, that they let their son and his wife live together in one room on the floor with Ranakandriana, their daughter.

But one day, Rafaravavy said to her husband, "I want to play with a horse." When he heard that, he said, "I'll do everything you want me to do if I can prove my love, even if I must go very far away from the village."

So he ordered his servants to go with him and they left to find a horse. However, when his parents heard that, they became jealous and thought, "This woman will cause our son's death by pushing him to go far away for her wishes."

So they decided to kill Rafaravavy by giving her some alcohol to drink. They went to visit her and stealthily brought a small bottle. By this time, Ranakandriana, their daughter, knew her parents would kill her sister-in-law, and she informed Rafaravavy and ordered her not to open the door but to reinforce the lock when they came. When they came, they knocked at the gate and Rafaravavy said, "I know you are coming to kill me by giving me some alcohol."

"No, we are not here to kill you. We would just like to visit with you," the parents said.

"You're lying," Rafaravavy said, and reinforced the locks of the seven walls separating them. But the parents destroyed all the locks and entered the room. They forced Rafaravavy to taste the drink and poured some on her lips and she died. After she died, the villagers buried her in the path where her husband usually walked.

Meanwhile in the woods, her husband, Randrianoro, had a nightmare and said to his servants, "Let's go back home. I had a dream and I know there's something wrong at home." So they returned.

When he was back, the people told him that his wife had been killed by his parents and she was already buried in the usual way. He was so sad and wept and wept. He went to his wife's grave, but when he destroyed the grave and opened it to see her, he was very surprised and amazed to see his wife wake up and come to life again. Then he was so happy that he could do nothing but weep some more.

After they had been reunited for some days, Rafaravavy told her husband, "I'd like to come to my father's house because I miss my parents."

Randrianoro replied, sadly, "Let me come with you. I love you very much and I will miss you. I won't be able to do anything."

But his wife told him, "No, you won't be able to stand my father's conditions."

"I'll do everything he wants. Don't worry."

And since Rafaravavy could not convince her husband to stay, she finally let him follow her to heaven. However, before leaving the earth, she advised him not to sit in the north corner of the room but in the south corner. And Randrianoro was told to gather every bird and animal that ever existed and trust them to help him if ever he needed them. And the birds and animals agreed to help him when they were gathered up. Finally, Randrianoro had followed everything his wife had ordered him to do, and they left for her father's house.

When they arrived in heaven, Rafaravavy's father said, "So you want to marry my daughter?" As he spoke, the thunder burst.

"Yes sir, I would have her for my wife," Randrianoro told him.

"Well, you will have to plow my large rice field first. Then, you have to fell the huge tree in the middle of the playground. Third, you have to know, among these thousand cows, which is the mother. And finally, my three daughters and their mother have the same faces. You must tell me who is the mother."

Randrianoro agreed to do whatever he was asked. When he had finished with plowing the rice field and felling the tree, he called the cows, and the birds. The flies promised him that the one which had a fly on top of her nose would be the mother, and the first one who had a fly on her head would be the three daughters' mother.

Randrianoro finished all of his chores and his father-in-law was amazed. He was also so happy that he blessed the young people and said that they would become husband and wife in his eyes forever, and be happy forever.

And when Randrianoro and Rafaravavy came back to the earth again, he cursed his parents, and said he didn't want to live with them any more, and wouldn't give them anything. And so the parents were poor and left alone.

—as told by Mme. Victoria
(Betafo)

CHAPTER IV

SPIRITS OF WATER,
SPIRITS OF LAKES

Lake Tritriva was truly magical. There is no other way to explain why I risked the trip in a stripped-down Peugeot on a road lined with laughing goats and mocking children. I have this little quirk of believing a car needs a road, something reasonably continuous and—left to my own decisions—reasonably flat. Not hairpin curves that end at the cliff's edge, not a series of gulleys connected by clumps of dirt. Understand, I have seen questionable routes before. On the Isle of Majorca, my car sped past groves of gnarled olive trees, twisted tree limbs mimicking the road's cul-de-sacs and curves. The sea, crested with bejeweled waves, waited for me at the end of that ride. But in Madagascar, the road to Tritriva was all gravel and thistle, and on the dry volcanic slope of the mountain, I began to believe the lake itself was a myth, a figment of someone's imagination.

We had come the back way, which suggests that there is a direct route. Such is not the case. To reach Tritriva from either the north or the west, you must take a route that carries you over twenty-five miles of rocky terrain—the going so cautious, travel time is doubled. As we chugged along, dust parachuting out behind us, the zebu warned us, flicking their ears against their horns when we passed as if to say: "You will wish for our help when the going gets tough." But even before the road took us onto the steeper slopes, I knew the going was tough. The goats agreed, shaking their heads at the sight of strangers who didn't have the good sense to abandon the car and take to the road on foot.

We jiggedy-hicked past a scattering of farmhouses that were bricked in rust colored adobe, tall and narrow as New York walk-ups. We passed terraced rice fields interspersed by fallow fields where volcanic rock jutted up from spiky grass as if the lava had stopped mid-spurt and ended in a domed hump. "Elephant rock," we had called it back home in St. Louis when the grade school class visited the zoo. The steep grade clutched the rim of steeper hills, and the valley, several hundred feet below, was clay red and bright green—fertile patches checkered with slashes of blood red laterite where rain had washed away the topsoil and left a gash of raw earth in the pattern of rice paddies. Above us, the sky dreamed in watercolor streaks of blue pinched narrow by fingers of white clouds, all of it made more intense by the backdrop of sun. But the road seemed to ignore any pattern, natural or man-made. It disappeared capriciously into ravines only to reemerge and grab an axle or snatch a wheel out of whack. The Peugeot saved us. Without upholstery and little amenities like door handles and floor covering, it was all-metal and mean as a stallion. I began to have fond memories of all the back roads I'd traveled in Guatemala and Yugoslavia, where I had survived donkeys and twisting corkscrews with cusps that held the skeletons of cars. Tritriva's road contained no graveyards of lost cars, and no one passed by on donkeys, both passenger and pack mule glancing my way with bemused looks. Aside from goats, dragonflies, and an occasional clustering of zebus, we were alone.

When we stopped to repair road damage—at least five or six times along the way—Tiana and I would stand to the side while Haingo, Serge, and the driver performed surgery on the beast. When we were inside, the car made rumbling noises to warn us that its heart wasn't in the climb, but whenever we stopped to fix some malfunction, the Peugeot lost its malevolence and looked like a normal car, ready for a weekend outing. I wasn't fooled. We seemed to spend more time outside of the car than inside. Every half mile or so, something would give way, and once we passed the point of no return, we were left to the mercy of the Peugeot. I'd like to say the excitement of nearly reaching our destination overcame my fear of being stranded on that road, but by the time everyone began to assure me that the end was near, I was all too sure the end was near. We'd navigated one curve too many, had slid once too often to the edge, one wheel spinning in the dusty air while the other three desperately gripped the slope. But somehow, by the grace of the ancestors, we arrived.

When the Peugeot finally pulled us up the last warp and weft of that road, the goats, staring in amazement, were joined by children who seemed to appear out of nowhere. They danced along the hillside beside us, as nimble as the very air itself. They greeted us as if we were the lead car in a sideshow come to set up tents. "*Akory e! Akory e!*" "Hello, hello," they laughed, surefooted among rocks and red flower thornbushes. How could they make it look so easy? I slumped in the seat, my fear dissolving into humility. Then, I pulled myself from the Peugeot and looked up.

Behind us, the road had vanished at last, leaving in its wake a goat track of pale dirt zigzagging toward a line of evergreens, flung like a mantle at the top of the path. If I closed my eyes for a second, I could imagine myself back in the Pacific Cascades, except the sun beat down with equatorial heat, and steam from the Peugeot's radiator smelled of metallic red clay. I was only a few steps up the path when I realized how well that car had shielded me from the sun's rays. Several children noisily vied to be the one who would sell me a hat. I chose a sisal derby woven in the patterns of the nearby village. The young girl who sold it to me was pleased that I had selected her work. She smiled and pointed to the tree line at the top of the ridge. "*Fariby*," she said, "The lake," as if to tell me the lake had been expecting me. With the hat shielding me from the sun, I scanned the line of trees. Under a tall pine at the top of the path, the storyteller was waiting.

Madagascar was dotted with lakes, each of them, it seemed, yielding stories of water monsters, beautiful sirens, and star-crossed lovers. At Lake Andraikiba, not far from Tritriva, legend has it that on a special night, there are those who can see the girl who drowned trying to please her lover, the king, by swimming across the lake when she was pregnant. It is said that you can see her in the very first rays of dawn, but it is forbidden to speak to her, or to let silk touch the waters of that lake lest she perish forever. In Toliara, I had watched a dance troupe perform a song-poem about the enchantment of a water sprite who leaves the lake but must return before she loses her beauty. So she lures a lover close to the water and seduces him with the radiance of her hair, "filled with water that glows like a thousand jewels." And in the north, near Antsiranana (Diégo Suarez), the legend of sacred lakes tells of the water spirit who was kidnapped by the king, but she was so beautiful, he surrendered himself to her watery kingdom rather than live without her. And then there was the legend of Tritriva.

The storyteller led us to a lookout point above the lake. There, we could see Tritriva in its entirety. It was the proper setting for the story: the water cupped in the mouth of the crater, the storyteller bringing the lovers to life as the trees swayed into the wind. He was an older man, grizzled in appearance and wearing a weather-beaten straw hat. He looked more like a farmer than the keeper of the lake and its legend. He stood under a tamarind tree and began to tell us about the lake.

"He has told this to visitors many times before," Haingo said. The leaves seemed to whisper, "yes, yes," as the wind ruffled them.

All the way up the mountain, I had noticed the air growing thinner. Now I realized I could take a deep breath of air so crisp, light and shadow seemed to flutter each time I inhaled. Was it the magic of the legend?

To hear the story of Tritriva while looking at the lake itself was like being caught in a hologram—you stand aside, watching yourself take it all in. The waters were sea coral blue and green, so still and clear that even the shape of the smallest leaves seemed to be the mirror image of something beneath the surface rather than mere shadows. The lake was trapped in a bowl of stone, its shoreline of steep cliffs rising abruptly out of the blue-green waters. Even standing directly above the lake, it seemed

Storyteller, Lake Tritriva

distant, out of reach, approachable only to those who dared to scale the escarpment.

It was Tiana's first visit to Tritriva, and like me, she was caught up in its enchantment. "I want to put my feet in the water," she said. "I want to say that I have been in the place of lovers."

I looked at the thin straps of the gold beach sandals she was wearing. "Those aren't exactly hiking shoes," I said. "And I don't want to read headlines in tomorrow's paper: Beautiful Translator Killed at Tritriva."

She kept staring at the sheer drop of the cliffs, but in the end, we both settled for the magic in the story the caretaker offered. And below us, Lake Tritriva glowed like a perfectly faceted emerald in a well of volcanic rock. The ghosts of the lovers shadowed the trees at the water's edge as the storyteller explained how, for the sake of love, they had surrendered themselves to a watery death. "And all follows thusly," he said.

"For the Malagasy, these lovers are Romeo and Juliet," Tiana told me. "The king, when he heard about their deaths, was very unhappy and he found their parents guilty of their deaths. He says it is told so that no one should keep lovers apart."

"And all follows thusly," I said, and stared into the shadows dancing in the emerald green waters.

> *Tsara Doany Manonga Arivo*
> In a good palace, one feels the
> presence of the old warriors.
> MALAGASY PROVERB

കൗകൗകൗകൗ

The Legend of Tritriva

Once, there was no lake in that place. In the East, there was a kind of valley where a nobleman lived with his family. His name was Andriamparazato (the last of the hundred noblemen). One day, he had a nightmare, a vision which foretold that something was going to happen. He took his family away, moved behind the hill and lived in a village called Anjanampara (in the village of last sons). After they had barely settled in, the volcano erupted and the lava covered the opposite side of the new village. It was after that eruption that the lake appeared and the land took the same shape as the country of Madagascar. Later this place became a historical place, since it was there the two lovers committed suicide.

The young man called himself Rabeniomby (zebu's rich owner). He came from Ingaina in the north upland of Betafo and eighteen kilometers from Tritriva, the lake itself; and the young woman was from the south upland of Betafo (many roofs), where the young woman's mother is still buried. These young people became lovers, but their parents did not give their approval to the marriage because they were arguing about family honor and position in the kingdom. One day, as the lovers had a tryst near that lake, they decided to drown themselves in the waters. They did and died there. Some time after their suicide, two small trees grew, their roots entwined, binding each other in the heart of the lake, symbolizing the two lovers who entered the water just under the trees. Even today, these trees are called the lovers' trees. It is said that this is a true story and is passed down for all to hear.

—as told at Lake Tritriva

ৡৡৡৡৡ

Rafara—Girl of the Waters

Today I come and I recall. This is what the old ones say. The water girl lived in an enchanted house at the bottom of the Green Waters. She had long hair, the color of fire. Rafara was her name and her small slave was called Ikala. One day they escaped to play on the rosy sand at the water's shore. As they played, Andriambohoaka glimpsed them, and he wanted to seize the Girl of the Green Waters. But he could not seize her because she rushed back into the waters, followed by her slave.

Andriambohoaka was truly sad to see them leave. He returned to his palace on the hill, and the next day went to see the sorcerer, Raininka-tombi, and asked him to make a *skidy*, a sorcerer's spell, for him.

But Raininkatombi said, "Father, prosperity attends you, yet you seem disturbed. What is it, my son?" [Here "father" and "son" are terms of friendship rather than of blood kinship.]

"I have seen there at the water's edge two pretty girls, and I would be happy to take one of them for my wife. But they disappeared and the waters closed over them."

Raininkatombi questioned the grains of *sikidy*, then he said, "Yes my son, these are the girls who live on the water's floor and look for kindness. If you have not been kind, you will not have what you desire."

"What must be done then?" said Andriambohoaka.

"Look closely. The cost will be revealed by the black cock who has never sung and by five pieces of money."

"Good," said Andriambohoaka.

"Here is the omen then," said Raininkatombi. "You must hide yourself near the sand where they play, and when you see they have let themselves dry, throw yourself on them and seize them by the hair."

Andriambohoaka hid himself near the beach. After a while, the Girl of the Green Waters and her slave left the water. He watched them for a long time, and when he saw they were not wet, he approached them carefully and seized them by the hair. "I desire to take you for my wife," Andriambohoaka told Rafara. She did not respond, and he almost lost courage until he remembered that she was mute. So he took Rafara and Ikala with him, and joined his people.

The people asked him, "Who is her father? Who is her mother? Where did she come from?"

Andriambohoaka had no answer for all of the questions. And Rafara and Ikala continued not to speak. They remained silent as stones, or tombs, or dead trees. The people went down the hill from the palace, each one shaking his head. And after being married for some time, Rafara assumed the world of men and had a child.

One day, when Andriambohoaka was in the rice fields, the child began to cry. His mother held him in her arms and rocked him, singing:

O small one, fragment of my life, my love
Ravelonahana, Ravelonahana
hush . . . hush . . .

Her voice echoed like a small bell. A slave of Andriambohoaka's heard her, and when the king returned home from the rice fields, she crept to him and whispered, "O master, when you were in the rice fields, and while I was warming my poor self in the sun near the cattle pens, I heard your wife singing. She speaks when you are not there, and her voice is similar to a bell or the tinkle of coins."

"You swear this? She really sang?"

"Yes," she said. "I swear she was singing."

Arriving at the palace, Andriambohoaka hid in the straw very near Rafara and Ikala. When the child was in the cradle, the mother began to sing. When he heard this, Andriambohoaka leapt from his hiding place in the straw and cried, "O Rafara, you can talk when you do not see me!" But she remained mute. He caressed her, and pleaded with her to speak, but she did not respond. Despite his threats, she remained mute. Then he beat her, as a disobedient wife. Rafara did not speak, but big tears ran from her eyes. A terrible noise was heard, and Andriambohoaka saw with horror that the tears formed a torrent that roared their way down the hill toward the Green Waters. And on this stream of tears, Rafara and Ikala plunged into the house of her father.

Andriambohoaka took the child from her arms as she fled him. He tried to pursue his wife beyond the water's edge, calling, "Rafara, child-of-the-waters, Rafara, child-of-the-waters. Return and I will give you all that is precious in this world—my firstborn, my youngest, my father, my mother."

Rafara answered, "O Andriambohoaka, the firstborn and youngest, you say? The father and the mother? Those are no presents for me."

Andriambohoaka rushed in the direction where her voice came and cried, "Rafara, Rafara, child-of-the-waters, I will give you my firstborn, the youngest, my father and mother, a hundred slaves and a million cattle."

Rafara answered, "The firstborn, the youngest, your father and mother, a hundred slaves and a million cattle? Those are no gifts for me."

During this time, Rafara and Ikala had not yet arrived at the bottom of the Green Waters. A big cayman, with one dismal eye, which he let float on the surface of the water, surveyed his surroundings.

Cayman, o blue cayman
Sleeping are you distracted?
When the girl-of-the-waters arrived
Is the door not open before her?

The cayman, who guarded the first enclosure of coral, was very surprised to hear this voice. He approached the water's edge. The girl-of-
the-waters and her slave mounted his back and thus they passed the
first enclosure and the seven enclosures that opened before them and
closed again. And all the small and large caymans with their scaly backs
were watching them pass. They said joyously to one another, "Is it possible? The Girl of the Green Waters has returned?"

"Yes," said the big cayman with one dismal eye. "It is she. I recognize her."

Meanwhile, Andriambohoaka, on the riverbank, continued his
lament:

Rafara, child-of-the-waters,
Come back. Come back, I say.
Your husband is sad.
Your child is miserable.

He cried for a long time. Two caymans, who were several centuries
old, left the water that carried them. They were sent by Rafara's parents.
Andriambohoaka said to them, "If I enter the water with my child, we
could not breathe and we would die."

But the biggest cayman replied, "Have no fear. You will not be sick.
We are here."

Andriambohoaka and his child plunged into the water and were not
made wet. They followed the cayman for a long time. Then an enchanted palace appeared before them. Rafara came to greet them. She
spoke and her voice sang. Numerous slaves followed, dressed like her in
their long hair.

The king-of-the-waters and his wife were very happy and welcomed Andriambohoaka and the child. The two lived like this for many years. And I let this story of their happiness remain, for the words have left my head and the tale was never to be finished.

—as told in Antsiranana
(Diégo Suarez)

CHAPTER V

ROCK, PAPER, SCISSORS

The town of Fianarantsoa in the Highlands of Madagascar is cradled in the saddleback massifs of the Kianjasoa, a rugged mountain range that rises, bare and stark as monoliths, into foggy mist hanging as delicate as babies'-breath above them. That was my first view: hills that were formed from huge stones studded with a smattering of trees, and a frosting of mist that softened the view. Under this fringe of clouds, everything surrounding Fianarantsoa seemed complicated, mysterious, and unpredictable.

I remember the town as a collection of churches and castle-like nunneries, one of the world's oddest hotels, and the sudden appearance of road bandits waiting at the outskirts of town as if they suspected that anyone leaving Fianar had to be carrying treasures. Certainly by the end of that trip, I left with a wealth of memories of Fianarantsoa—that "place of good learning," as the name translates to English—an enchanting landscape where graceful women wove lambas and made paper embossed with wildflowers. It was a place of artists and scholars, storytellers and musicians. It was, Haingo had told me, a place where international researchers and naturalists rested on their way south to the Berenty Wildlife Reserve to study the flora and fauna, or on their way to Isalo, where rock formations resembled stalagmites pulled from ancient caves now laid bare to the sky.

The countryside around Fianar held the first traces of that magnificant landscape, the town adorned with great bare stones that rose against the skyline like the backs of slumbering bullocks. Roads were cut to navigate around those stones. I spent a lot of time making a mental map of routes, sometimes my head spinning from simply trying to remember what direction a circular street would take, or, in the case of Hotel Soafia, what direction I needed to take on the simple journey from my room to the reception desk. The design of the Soafia was as complicated as the layout of Fianar, its interlocking pagodas not unlike the town's three levels of circular districts rising up endlessly winding streets. I might have spent my whole visit navigating my way through Fianar if Tiana hadn't introduced me to Simon Ramarijaona before we left the capital city.

I had been walking in the Zoma market with Tiana when Simon called to her. She remembered him from the days when he drove a taxi near the university. "Now he has his own car," she said. We talked, this Simon who owned a car, who looked enough like Robert Townsend, the African American actor and film director, to have been his brother—slightly built with a boyish face, a pencil thin mustache, and a ready smile to match his wry humor. But best of all, the car, a Renault, was as handsome as Simon, and it had brakes that worked, a regular gas tank instead of a plastic bottle near the accelerator as some taxis had, and a driver who loved speed but didn't have the need to face death on every curve. Simon also loved his car. He wanted to keep it clean, polished, and in one piece. I loved his car, but that was because I could rent the whole thing for Tiana, Haingo, and myself for the length of the trip instead of riding like cargo slapped cheek-to-jowl in a taxi-brousse or minibus. If there was any flaw in this arrangement, it was that we left Antananarivo with only one audiotape. (At least Simon, unlike the inimitable Serge, had a tape player.) I heard *Ankalazao ny Tompo* [*Praise to God*] replayed so often that by the time we returned from the trip, I almost knew the tune by heart. But I didn't care. Simon and his car were dependable.

We left the capital just after dawn when the early morning light still bleached the houses lining the hillside opposite La Karthala. Simon sped away from Tana as if National Highway 7 suddenly had been transformed into the wide lanes of an autobahn. By midday, we cleared the fertile valley near Antsirabe and sped south toward the moonscape of plateau country and scrub forests. Simon slowed only for villages that appeared abruptly, and were full of houses hugging the road like hitchhikers. In the larger towns along the National Highway, people paid so little attention to the car that some did not move until the absolutely last minute. But as the road narrowed, we passed a scattering of dirt villages where the inhabitants, dressed in well-worn lambas and straw hats for work in the rice fields, turned to stare into the car windows, surprised to see something other than a taxi-brousse or a minibus.

This was the countryside of zebu carts and horses; those with private cars could only be passing through. Houses were built Highland style — slender two-story pitched roof structures that reminded me of the architecture of "railroad houses" in some parts of the midwestern region of the U.S., houses designed for railroad workers and given that nickname because their width, reminiscent of a train compartment, accommodated only one room for each floor. On the moonscape terrain of Madagascar's Highlands, those houses seemed impossibly tall, standing unadorned in treeless yards — "dirt plain," my grandmother would have said — their bright red clay walls glowing in the sunlight like beacons.

As we headed farther south, red dust began to tint everything, from houses to plants to the lambas draping the shoulders of farmers. Along the road, a young boy, selling carrots and potatoes, proudly posed for me with a basket of his produce. After kneeling for hours waiting for a car to stop, his knees were coated with dust. When we stopped for gas and coffee at a roadside turnout, dust and bugs tried to invade our car, some of both floating inside before I could shut the door. A poor man, lame in one leg, approached the car with his hand out for money. His skin, his ragged pants, and the lamba draped around his shoulder all assumed

Vegetable seller on the road to Fianarantsoa

the same color as the dusty road. He saw my camera and shook his head, but when I said, "Les francs pour votre photographie," he smiled. Farther down the road, we bought roasted ears of corn and bright orange tangerines. We ate them as *Ankalazao ny Tompo* played again and again. When the tape was rewinding, Tiana, Simon, and Haingo debated the upcoming elections and the political situation in Madagascar—a situation, given the continuing economic depression of the country, that was tenuous at best.

"More than a hundred candidates are vying for fifty-eight parliamentary seats," Tiana said. "We will hear the propaganda for the rest of this month."

"Political speeches?" I asked.

"Yes, the speech of political propaganda," she said.

I thought about the two-party system in the U.S. and the many speeches that flaunted one point of view while deriding all others. Propaganda seemed like a more reasonable term than speech, but the situation in Madagascar was a tangle of political intrigue in which I was easily lost without my usual landmarks of liberal-conservative slogans. I listened to their debate and *Ankalazao ny Tompo* with only half an ear. On flat-out stretches, I dozed, but when we neared the hills of Fianarantsoa, I awakened as the Renault labored uphill past a panorama of rice paddies and fruit vineyards dotted with stones.

We arrived in Fianar in late afternoon as the sun, filtered through mist, washed the houses in bloodstreaks of light and cast the shadows of vineyards into darker shades of green. At some intersections the road circled around humps of stones, part of the outer reaches of the Kianjasoa massifs, scattered through the town. We entered Fianar just as it was transforming itself from the work of the day to the rhythms of evening. Along hilly streets the *Hotely*, or small diners, some that were no more than part of a narrow room with a bench table and a few stools, were doing a bustling business of quick snacks: bowls of rice or beans, and cups of thick sweet coffee. Upscale restaurants like Chez Papillon were already crowded, mostly with tourists—foreigners who came to Fianar to study its vineyards, crafts, and geological formations. And there were the Christians, both Catholic and Protestant, who had strongholds in Fianar. Certainly there were churches in the capital city, Tana, but in Fiana-rantsoa there seemed to be a larger number of church steeples rising above the skyline of one- and two-story buildings. And often, like the stones of Kianjasoa, the churches created little cul-de-sacs that caused detours in the road. I learned to use them as landmarks—the Protestant church here, the Catholic church there—to signal whether I was in Upper Town, New Town, or Lower Town.

We drove along a spiraling street into the Lower Town area of Fianar. With the early evening light blurring corners and curves, the ride was dizzying, full of intersections where roads crisscrossed themselves to avoid the obstructions set down by nature. The route twisted into the valley where rough cobblestones threatened to break the shocks on the Renault. I began to long for the visible crevices in the dirt roads near Lake Tritriva, the kind a driver could avoid. Fianar's roads were uniformly hard and unyielding, like the stones of Kianjasoa. They blocked the flow of water. In fact, the lack of drainage had forced the hotel we were looking for to close its doors temporarily. When we finally found it, at the far end of Lower Town, we stumbled into an entry hall that was ankle-deep in mud. A girl was halfheartedly swabbing the floor, moving the mud around more than clearing it out. "Come in," she gestured, but that was easier said than done.

"A flood," Tiana said. "They are still cleaning up from the rainy season." We would have to go elsewhere to find shelter for the night. And so, the Renault made the laborious climb back uphill, then down again to another section of town. The second hotel, a walkup close to the cattle market, was like some place sliced from the warehouse district of Kansas City, or port towns like Norfolk, Virginia. I was rather relieved that it was booked solid, but that put us on the road again, descending another coil of streets to the district where the incomparable Hotel Soafia awaited us.

By the time we arrived at the Soafia, it was already dark and we had been traveling all day. Still, my first glimpse of the place gave me reason to pause. There, in the heart of Madagascar, was a Chinese pavilion, complete with sloping roofs made of curved tiles, winged eaves, tiered balconies, and intersecting pergolas, all of it lacquered red and trimmed in gold. Bronzed lions, turned corrosive green by rain, offered their silent roars at the entryway. A huge brass gong hung in the archway leading to the garden. The architecture was so different from anything else I'd seen in Madagascar that I stood there, openmouthed.

"Many researchers stay here," Haingo said. "It is world famous."

"I don't doubt it," I said. The Soafia spread out in all directions like a painting unfolding on an enormous ceremonial kimono. We had arrived at dusk, and the outside lights, reflected off the waters of the ornamental pool, danced like yellow candle flames. I half expected someone to sound the gong to announce the entrance of strangers. Tiana and Simon came out of the reception hall with the news that, happily, the Soafia had room for us. "And a couple of dynasties too," I said.

Simon unloaded our bags and left us to the mercy of the Soafia. I looked longingly after the car as its taillights vanished into the direction of Simon's family. Haingo patted me on the shoulder, but I wasn't comforted as we followed the bellhop down the corridor—well, not exactly down the corridor because that implies a straight line. The dragon that had designed the Soafia had carved the corridors in the shadow of its tail. It wasn't a hallway; it was a serpent's lair that ran for what seemed like miles into a subterranean passage away from Reception. We followed the bellhop like obedient ducks, turning right, turning left, turning right, ever onward.

"Where's the room?" I asked. Tiana translated. The bellhop pointed vaguely to the space ahead of us. We turned right, turned left, turned right. I realized I couldn't remember how many right turns we'd taken. There was only one corridor and no windows to mark our way. Only rooms with unnumbered doors painted red.

"Where is the dining room?" I asked. Tiana translated. The bellhop pointed to the distance behind us.

"Where is the exit?" I asked. Haingo translated. The bellhop pointed to the distance behind us.

"Is there room service?" I asked. Tiana laughed. Haingo translated. The bellhop pointed to the only direction he seemed to favor—the mysterious land of the reception desk.

We'd been walking for five minutes through the unchartered forest of Chinese red doors before I yelled, "Stop!" and pointed to the distance behind us. The bellhop didn't need any translation.

Reception was another matter. "The rooms are perfectly good," the clerk said. "I'm sure they are," I said, "but I didn't bring my roller skates." The clerk sighed. Finally, we settled on rooms near the road, where I had to stuff towels in the windows to keep out the diesel fumes from passing trucks. The beds creaked, the rugs were gummy Chinese red, and the walls some indescribable variation on eastern brocade, but there was comfort in knowing the exit was nearby and visible. One step into the hallway, and I could see the promised land of the reception desk.

What better home base to set out collecting stories of myth than the Hotel Soafia. The very act of finding the Soafia was cloaked in the mythology of a quest for stories. After all, booking into the Soafia on our third attempt to find a hotel in Fianar was not unlike following the course of a good folktale: success always came with that magical number—three. It gave me license to expect the unexpected. And in a country where orchids and ylang-ylang grew from a landscape of boulders and scrub pine, a Chinese pagoda, with its ornate pavilions and peaked roofs, must have been spawned from someone's myth. So I started the next day bright with the promise of contacting storytellers. The magic of the Soafia did not let me down. In the dining room, almost completely occupied by foreign researchers, among them several Americans from Tana whom I recognized, we had the Soafia's breakfast of watery Tang (a common Malagasy substitute for orange juice), weak cocoa, and a dry croissant that made me miss the long, crusty baguettes and tea Mme. Arianne offered at La Karthala. We'd just finished eating when Simon arrived with his father.

I instantly liked Philibert Ramarijaona, a retired gentleman who greeted me warmly. "He has lived here all of his life," Tiana translated, "and he has many people for us to see."

"Enchanté," I said. "Tell him I'd like to meet women storytellers, if it is possible."

"There are many in this area," Haingo said. "Perhaps M. Ramarijaona can show us the way."

Simon's father answered. "He is happy to have the time to spend with you," Tiana translated.

Where Simon appeared to be as lithe as a dancer in tan slacks and a polo shirt, his father seemed fragile, his overcoat buttoned to the collar although the weather was mild. But his mannerisms were not frail. He immediately began to give directions, explaining where we were to go and why, and Simon, the obedient son, moved quickly to follow them. The five of us crowded into Simon's car and set off to explore Fianarantsoa. M. Ramarijaona explained the layout of the town, its three districts spreading out from Mount Kianjasoa like a fan. He liked poetry and, impressed that I was a poet, took us to a school—part of a university, he said. It was a Byzantine-like building attached to a convent and hospital. The school, built from the stones of Kianjasoa, was as solid and imposing as the convent. The sprawl of buildings all but choked off the street, leaving a narrow one-car lane road that almost came to a dead end near the steps of the main building. But on the ramparts at the top of the steps, I could see clear into the valley. I couldn't locate the Hotel Soafia from that distance, but I knew it was there, with its serpentine halls and stone lions. Haingo checked with the school to inquire whether a couple of local poets were still in town. "I think we'll find them tomorrow," he said. Both

M. Ramarijaona and I smiled at the promise of success. When we left the school, he led us to an area near the Route de Corniche, where, he said, the renowned papermakers of Fianarantsoa could be found.

We drove into the hills along a maze of streets sandwiched between garden paths and lean-tos. At the bottom of a steep incline, we left Simon with the car and walked up a stairstep street to a wooded lot that held several open-air sheds. Two or three children came out to greet us, and then a young man, who apparently knew M. Ramarijaona, joined them. Simon's father shook hands with the man and with several others who had taken a moment from their work in the sheds. Tiana introduced me to all of them, and Haingo explained why we were visiting. "This is where they make the paper," Haingo told me. As I walked toward the sheds, the men explained the process of creating bark paper. The business was owned by the Razanatsara family, and by the looks of them, most of the men were relatives. They had the same brown complexion and round faces that reminded me of people I'd met on visits to Southeast Asia. They were people of the Highlands—Betsileo—and somewhat less obviously connected to African ancestry than the Bara, Mahafaly, and Sakalava people I'd met when visiting the coastal areas of Madagascar. Their slender fingers seemed suited for the delicate work of papermaking.

They led me from one shed to the next—the soaking shed, the press shed, the pattern shed, the drying tables—an Old World process very similar to the method of making papyrus. As I moved from one shed to the next, the paper appeared as if by magic out of the pulp of the inner lining of tree bark. After it began to lose the markings of its natural fiber in the soaking shed, it was spread out to dry, yellowing as it took on the cast of paper. The paper came out in thin sheets, almost transparent but with bits of bark still visible, like the shadows of veins under the skin. In the last stages, just before the drying tables, the petals of wildflowers and ferns were added to create designs. Each sheet was unique, a beautifully crafted screen that almost seemed pulled from a garden, bouquets of

Young papermaker, Fianarantsoa

flowers artfully arranged as if in a vase. The pattern of flowers in that final stage reflected the artistry and craft of the designer.

"No two pieces are exactly alike," Haingo said. "So even with many papermakers in the area, some are more in demand than others. The paper is used for decoration. For wall coverings and boxes. And of course, for writing notes and making invitations for special occasions."

I watched a beautiful young woman work with flowers: blue cactus blooms and precious periwinkles, placing them on the wet parchment petal by petal, balanced atop bits of fern, thin as silk thread, and small spiderwebbed leaves. The woman was expecting a baby, and her face held the glow that some pregnant women get when they're in the late stages of sharing life with the infant. I asked if I could take her picture. She nodded shyly, but never looked directly into the lens. When I raised the camera, she blushed and I had the pose I wanted: her brown face bent to her work, her hair piled in a mass of thin delicate braids, gathered on her head like a crown. Her skin was luminescent in the sunlight reflected off the sheets of newly formed paper. How like a Madonna she seemed at that moment.

While I watched the beautiful papermaker at work, the children watched me. I was the *vazaha*, the foreigner. As I walked through the workshop, the children listened to Haingo and Tiana translate for me. They stared with that idle curiosity that all children have, a look that asked: Have you come to see us or the grown-ups?

"Bonjour. Ça va?" I said, and they giggled at the American accent riding through my French.

"They don't speak French," Tiana told me.

"It's better than my Malagasy," I said.

She told the children what I'd said, and they giggled even more. Then they ran toward the house. I hadn't noticed, but while I was touring the paper sheds, M. Ramarijaona had entered the house. When we reached the door, he was waiting for us with an older woman.

"Their mother," Tiana said, introducing Mme. Alphonsisme. The children lingered at the threshold but stayed just outside the door. Haingo also remained outside. "You have enough people to translate," he said. "I will talk to the papermakers."

I left him and followed Tiana. "She is from America," Tiana explained as we took our seats.

"I am delighted to be here," I said. "The paper is beautiful. Very delicate."

While Tiana translated, and M. Ramarijaona explained why we had come, Mme. Alphonsisme studied my face. We looked at each other and smiled. She was a small woman wearing a cotton housedress, its pattern of flowers all but faded from years of use. Still, I could not help but be reminded of the paper taking shape in the sheds outside. And with her round face and plump figure, I would not have had any difficulty identifying her as the mother of the children hovering around the door. The children were similar in appearance, but where they seemed mischievous, full of giggles and elbowing each other, Mme. Alphonsisme looked rather sad until she smiled, then her face brightened and a gold front tooth, a symbol of her family's prosperity, winked in the light. Evidence of the family's prosperity was all around us, from the compound of neatly ordered cottages spreading out from the hub of the family business, the papermaking sheds. I think I had expected to find the house decorated in bark paper designs, but in the small room where I sat with Mme. Alphonsisme, each wall was adorned with one or two movie posters, their size dwarfing a photograph of M. Albert Zafy, president of Madagascar. Two worlds in collision: the president of a country, and the celluloid icons of Hollywood.

Mme. Alphonsisme seemed to be caught up in a conversation with Haingo and M. Ramarijaona, but I could sense she was also watching me. "Arnold Schwarzenegger. Clint Eastwood," I said, paying homage to the posters. She grinned and her gold tooth picked up the light reflected off the glossy surface of the posters. They were all of action movies, the only ones U.S. distributors seemed to export to foreign countries. The America those countries saw was restricted by the camera's selective eye. Given those movies, I came from a place where most people owned an uzi, and lived in the heart of drug Mafia country that was rife with CIA agents and gangland wars. In Tana, I had tried to describe *Daughters of the Dust*, a film about the myth and history of the Georgia Sea Islands made by an African American woman director, Julie Dash.

"How could such a film exist," the students had said. Their exposure to American movies had included *Escape from New York*, *Die Hard*, and a multitude of American kung fu films. I told them how most Americans thought of Madagascar as a place where lemurs abounded, and man-eating plants, straight out of Marco Polo's "Isle of the Moon," waited for their victims. "Those are just stories," they said.

"So are the movies," I told them. They looked at me with skeptical eyes. What I meant to say was that on both sides of the ocean, the unknown world was shaped, for better or worse, by stories torn from bits and pieces of reality and tempered by the imagination. That's why I had come to Madagascar—to collect stories that reflected the culture and myths of the country. But I knew that the lives of most of the Malagasy people could not be measured in folktales where shapechangers rose from the sea and elephant birds darkened the sky with their great wings, any more than the lives of most Americans were modeled after the movies. Perhaps I was distressed that those icons which had traveled across the ocean did not include African American actors alongside their white counterparts. "Do they have any posters with Eddie Murphy or Spike Lee?" I asked Tiana.

Mme. Alphonsisme and M. Ramarijaona looked puzzled. "They are talking about stories," Tiana said. "Mme. Alphonsisme is a storyteller. She wants to know what you will do with the stories you have collected."

"Tell her that I am interested in traditional stories that are still being told, stories that are passed from one generation to the next." I was speaking to Tiana, but looking at Mme. Alphonsisme. We held each other's gaze for a while until she smiled again, seemingly satisfied with what she'd read in my face. I apologized for interrupting her day when there was so much work to do for the family and for the business of making paper. Mme. Alphonsisme smoothed the folds of her dress and nodded.

"She will give you some stories if we come back later, after she has finished her work," Tiana said. "But she is not really a storyteller. She can only repeat the stories she heard as a child."

"That is exactly what I want," I said. "In America, we call them 'grandmother stories.'"

Mme. Alphonsisme beamed. "She says she is a grandmother," Tiana translated. On the wall above Mme. Alphonsisme's left shoulder, Chuck Norris demonstrated his box kick.

We left Mme. Alphonsisme's just as the town was falling under the spell of the noonday sun. It was that time of the day when Madagascar seemed

to take on colors pulled from a box of primary paints: the sky unbelievably blue with a few cotton white clouds, the ground coated in red dust,
and everything in bloom. Trees were heavy with bright red flowers—
Thanksgiving palms, we called them back home—and gardens held
splashes of vivid purple, pink, and yellow blossoms. Wind stirred the grass,
leaving streaks of gold-green light, and the patterns of lambas on women
coming home from the market took on the vividness of a Degas painting.

Fianar may have been some distance from the capital, but it had the
same aura as Tana, a kind of urban flair that blended the business world
and country life. Everyone seemed to be rushing toward work or the next
appointment. Office workers on lunch break dodged farmers leading
cattle to market, and Malagasy cowboys on horseback herded zebu around
street vendors selling fresh produce. Straw hats carrying the geometry of
patterns from Antaimoro and Betsileo villages crowned the heads of most
passersby, while the all-purpose lamba draped the shoulders of everyone except the barefoot young boys who apprenticed themselves to run
errands for businesses. They seemed to be everywhere, those boys—
ragged, handsome, and eager to please—clamoring around pedestrians
and scooting through traffic. At times, the traffic was fierce, a tangle of
cars, taxi-brousses, bicycles, busses—not as dense as in Antsirabe, but the
obvious congestion of a city. But it was the foot traffic that most interested me, especially at the conjunction of streets near the train station in
Lower Town where we were having lunch. It was there, in front of Chez
Papillon, that I spotted two strolling musicians.

The decor at Chez Papillon was more Indonesian than Malagasy—
bamboo plants, beaded curtains, and a kind of sickly green paint. The
menu was a rather lackluster version of Malagasy-French cuisine, with
sauces that were a bit more intriguing than what the French offer, but
made more palatable by deliciously spiced fish, saffron rice, and the de-
light of local wine. It was a place where we could gather our thoughts
about the morning. We were all talking at once, thoroughly excited about
the prospect of Mme. Alphonsisme's stories. All through lunch, I had been

trying to urge M. Ramarijaona to offer some of his stories, but he claimed not to remember any. "He only lectures," Simon teased. So it was in that mood that we left Chez Papillon and stumbled onto the musicians.

When I saw them, they were across the street from the restaurant. They had just finished entertaining a small crowd and were about to move away from the Avenue du General Leclerc and closer to the train station on Route d'Ambalavao. I saw their instruments first—"the *jejy voatavo*," Haingo told me. The *jejy voatavo* were stringed like mandolins with heavy, round bellies the size of pumpkins, and long thin necks with knobbed struts that, from my vantage point across the street, resembled the intricately carved *aloalo* I'd seen on Mahafaly tombs. What caught my eye was the way the musicians held the instruments, belly-end nestled in the crook of the arm, the neck pointing downward. As they moved toward the station, they began to play again, just a few notes, a haunting sound like a serenade to a lost love.

Simon was holding open the car door, but I was transfixed, trapped in a melody that seemed to come from the wind, from the distant horizon where the Kianjasoa ridge rested under the purple haze of midday. In that moment, I think I was more "inside" Madagascar than I had been all day. I stood there, half in and half out of the car, inhaling the waxy scent of dust vying with the sharp odor of diesel fumes, while colors danced in the sunlight and incredibly haunting music wafted toward me. I must have said something. I'm not sure, perhaps not, but at that moment, Haingo said, "Stay here!" and darted across the street with M. Ramarijaona close at his heels. They conferred with the musicians, and after a bit of nodding and smiling, they all crossed the street. It had been agreed; they would play for us in the garden terrace in front of Chez Papillon. I recorded music of love and valor, of ancestors and the beauty of the land. Up close, the wood of the *jejy voatavo* was tawnier than that of pumpkins, more of a spiced brown hue like cedar with smooth contours, almost sensual, so that as they played, the light seemed to dance along the curves of wood in time with the music. The agility of the musician's right hand determined the pitch and timbre of the notes, and the *jejy voatavo* whispered the sounds of birds, of lemurs calling across a night forest of trees, of fish rippling the water. It was just the mood I needed to take with me back to Mme. Alphonsisme.

Simon dropped Tiana and me at the Razanatsaras and then, with Haingo for company, took his father home. It was dusk when we arrived, the light turning violet with the last rays of the sun, and the scent from cooking pots still hanging in the air. There was no one in the papermaking sheds; the canopies above the shelters billowed in the evening breeze. Tick birds chased insects in the fading light. I heard something calling in the voice of the katydid, but I had no Malagasy name for the sound or the bird. As we came up the path, the children saw us; they squealed with recognition and escorted us to the main house. Mme. Alphonsisme, wearing a dress adorned with bright blue periwinkles, came to the door. She seemed relieved to see that Tiana and I were alone.

"We will go to her house," Tiana said.

We followed her along the path until we came to a house that was identical to the others we had passed. The children would have come into the room behind us, but Mme. Alphonsisme stopped them at the door. Immediately, they began a game of run-and-chase and scampered into the shadows. I watched them, thinking of those early evenings in St. Louis when, as a child, I'd played similar games. It was the same kind of evening. A warm breeze rustled the bushes where insects were caroling their night songs, and the air was filled with high pitched laughter as one child inevitably found another, because there are only so many places to hide when you're at home. It was a perfect night for storytelling.

Tiana and I took our seats across the room from Mme. Alphonsisme. I told Tiana to ask her if I could take a few pictures before we began. Mme. Alphonsisme whispered her answer. I could barely hear her, and even Tiana, sitting closer to her than I was, had to lean forward.

Storyteller, Mme. Alphonsisme, Fianarantsoa

"She says yes," Tiana translated, "but she will only tell the stories if we turn out the lights."

I was a bit surprised, then I heard the laughter of the children playing in the yard, and remembered how I'd listened to stories in the half-dark when I was young. "Perfect," I said, and quickly took some photos before she turned off the lamp. On the wall behind her, I could barely see a shiny Hollywood poster of Rob Lowe, but in the magic of stories about kings and lovers and timid brides, his image seemed almost comical. And it was perfect to sit in that room and listen to stories which Mme. Alphonsisme herself had heard as a child. In the background, insects trilled the songs of the Highlands, and every now and then, the children's voices all but drowned Mme. Alphonsisme's shy narration. But the outside noises were merely moments of punctuation. We listened intently to Mme. Alphonsisme's stories. Her voice was enchanting with its singsong rhythm, the words rising and falling like the notes from the *jejy voatavo*.

We were on our way home from Fianar when we were accosted by bandits. I had been contemplating the feathery tops of pine trees when Simon came to such an abrupt stop that I thought we'd hit something. In another thirty feet or so, we would have. The trunk of a large tree had been placed across the road as a barrier. Seconds after we stopped, two men appeared—one crossing in front of the car, and the other behind us. I could see the heads of several more staring out at us from the bushes. The man near the front of the car walked toward us. He was a muscular fellow, his size accentuated by the tightness of his T-shirt, the sleeves of which had been torn off to reveal his biceps. But I was more interested in what he carried in his hand. It was a stick, short enough to be a cop's billy club but cruder, thicker. The first word that came to mind was "cudgel." The next word was "bandit."

"You will say nothing," Tiana whispered.

That was an unnecessary precaution. I had been struck dumb by the appearance of that cudgel, a word that must have come spiraling out of my dim memory of novels about old English road bandits, the highwaymen. Cudgel was not a word I used in any normal circumstances, but then, Malagasy road bandits, *dahalo*, weren't a part of any previous circumstances. Whatever the men were called, the weapon had the same effect. The bandit slapped the short stump of the stick against his palm. It was definitely a cudgel, I thought, as the sound echoed through the open window. As he questioned Simon, he peered into the back seat of the car. I willed every molecule of my body to appear Malagasy—Sakalava or Bara, I didn't care. It just wasn't a time to be *vazaha*. Simon took the man's questions easily, or at least he appeared to be at ease.

I heard Simon say, "Ambositra," and could only assume that he'd been asked where we'd come from, and had chosen to offer the last town we'd passed through as our place of origin. I thought I heard the word for father, and maybe for village, but Simon didn't let on that we were heading for Tana. Tana might have meant we were carrying something of value, something that could be translated into money. Then I remembered stories of how bandits had slaughtered everyone in a village, taking a few goats, lace doilies, and pictures off the wall, if there was nothing else of value. They had robbed trains near Toamasina (Tamatave), and pleasure boats off the coast near Mahajanga. And their methods seemed to have been fashioned after those of bandits of another era, sixteenth-century pirates who used Madagascar as their home away from home, especially when they were on the run from crimes committed on the high seas. Twentieth-century road bandits carried on that tradition of making capricious decisions to loot and ride on, or loot and kill. Their reputations were legendary, and it was not time for me to assert my presence as a foreign researcher.

"Look Malagasy," I thought, and crossed my fingers in hopes that the magical aura I'd picked up from the Soafia would serve me through this adventure as well. Then a minibus pulled up behind us, and the bandits turned their attention toward more lucrative prey. They waved us around the roadblock, and Simon floorboarded the Renault until we were out of sight over the next hill. I wanted to sound warnings, find the police, call out the militia. I wanted to find help for the passengers of the minibus, lodge a protest with the local authorities. "This is Madagascar," Tiana said. "We've been lucky. Now it is out of our hands." I couldn't just be silent, just slide past the outrageousness of bandits on the open road. "Too many movies," I said. "All those Westerns imported from America." My companions were silent. "What about the ancestors? Maybe they'll help," I said.

"They have," Haingo said. "We're back on the road again."

Akory ity adala miara-monina amin-kendry!
It is strange that an idiot
can live close by with the
wise.

ఆ ఆ ఆ ఆ ఆ

Raharinora and Randriantsara

Randriantsara was the son of a king. One day, he said to his parents, "Father, I want to go. Mother, I want to go."

"Why do you want to go?" asked his parents.

"There is a lady I love somewhere," answered Randriantsara.

"If you need a lady to love from somewhere, why don't you take one from here? There are several eligible ladies here, so you have no need to get one from far away."

"But I love this one," replied Randriantsara.

And so, Randriantsara left his parents and went to search for the lady he loved. He traveled for four days. Then he arrived at a city and knew this lady, Raharinora, lived there. He asked a passerby to show him her house.

"What is the purpose of your visit?" asked Raharinora's parents when Randriantsara arrived.

"I love your daughter," said Randriantsara.

"You love our daughter?"

"Yes," said Randriantsara.

"But I don't love him," Raharinora said.

"She does not love you, Randriantsara," the parents of Raharinora told him.

"Yes, she does," Randriantsara said. And he continued, "If you don't love me, I want to be hired as a worker for your father."

And so Randriantsara came to work for Raharinora's father. He worked there for a long time. After one year, Raharinora's father decided to give his daughter to Randriantsara.

"Here is your wife," said her father.

Raharinora accepted and said, "Whether I love him or I don't love him, I accept him as my husband. He has been a slave of my father's for a long time, and he is able to endure."

After they had been married for one year, Randriantsara told Ra-harinora, "I want to go home and take you with me. My mother and my father, I will carry your daughter home with me," Randriantsara said to Raharinora's parents.

And so, he took Raharinora to his home, but when she arrived, her parents-in-law hated her.

"Because of this girl, you went far away?" they asked Randriantsara.

"Yes," he replied.

But his parents were not happy with Raharinora, and because of that, Randriantsara told her that they had to find another place to live. They moved to the mountains and lived there. After living there for one year, Randriantsara said to his wife, "Because my father hates me now due to my love for you, I want to go far away to make money selling cattle from village to village."

Raharinora asked him, "What exactly do you want? You loved me very much and that is why you took me from far away. Why do you want to leave me and go far from me to sell cattle?"

"I will go to sell cattle to make money to be independent of my par-ents, because I see that you suffer very much," replied Randriantsara.

And so, Randriantsara left Raharinora and went far away. And Ra-harinora moved to the village where the parents of Randriantsara lived. But after a while, her parents-in-law planned to kill her because they were angry that their son had married her. They gathered the villagers and told them to call Raharinora to visit them.

The villagers went to the house where Raharinora lived and called out: "Raharinora! Raharinora! Go to meet your parents-in-law! Go! Go!"

Raharinora answered, "I'll come. I'll come to my parents-in-law."

When Raharinora arrived, her parents-in-law poured poison in her meal, and so when she returned to her house after eating from her parents-in-law, she had a stomachache.

Then the villagers called out: "Raharinora is ill!" And after a while, "Raharinora has died!"

After Raharinora died, the villagers said: "Her husband is not here but had gone far away to sell cattle. Let's bury her at the north of her house so that when her husband comes back, he will see her easily." The villagers kept the body of Raharinora for three days while waiting for her husband's return. On the fourth day of her death, they buried her.

Raharinora's husband did not know she was dead. When he returned to the town, he called out loudly from the riverbank: "Raharinora! Raharinora! Come to your husband by dugout canoe. I bring clothes for you. Come to your husband by dugout canoe. I bring jewelry made of gold for you." But Raharinora was dead and could not answer him.

"Let's go," said the boatman.

"I don't want to go if Raharinora does not come," replied Randriantsara.

"Raharinora will never come," the boatman told Randriantsara. "She is dead. Your father had a party and invited her. After she returned from the party, she became ill and died. She is already buried. Come, and I will show you the place where the villagers buried her."

After hearing that, Randriantsara got into the dugout canoe. When he arrived at the village, he called out: "Where is she buried? Where is my wife, Raharinora, buried?"

"Over there!" answered the villagers.

"Dig me a hole," Randriantsara said. "I want to commit suicide and be buried with Raharinora."

When the hole was dug, Randriantsara said, "Cover me with earth. I want to die like my wife."

And so they did. And from this time, it is customary to hear people saying: "Daughters-in-law are always hated by parents-in-law." And the people say it is so because Raharinora died from eating the food of her parents-in-law.

—as told by Mme. Alphonsisme
(Fianarantsoa)

Faralahy Mahery: Strong Youngest Son

Faralahy Mahery was a talented healer. There was a woman who wanted to have a child but she couldn't, so she went to see Faralahy Mahery. Faralahy Mahery said, "I'm going to heal you, sister. Bring your husband. But remember, when you have a baby, if it's a boy, he'll be my brother; but if she is a girl, she'll be my wife."

She brought her husband, and the woman and her husband agreed. When the woman gave birth, she had a baby girl. She sent a message to Faralahy Mahery to say, "I gave birth to a girl."

Faralahy Mahery said, "When she grows older, I'll come to get her to be my wife."

Days, months, and years went by, and the little girl grew up. And while playing with her playmates, they told her, "You can't play with us anymore because you're already married."

"Already married?" the girl asked.

"Yes, you are," her playmates answered. "As early as you were in your mother's womb, you were engaged to a man."

When they told her she was already married, the girl went home with tears rolling down her face. But as she grew older, she started asking her parents, "O my mother. O my father. Is it true that I'm already married?"

"Yes, you are," her parents answered. "You have been married since you were in your mother's womb. We could only have one child, thanks to Faralahy Mahery, and we promised him that if we had a boy, he would be his brother, but if it was a girl, she would be his wife once she grew older. That is why you have to marry him. Sooner or later, the time will come when he will return. Even though he is still away, we can't break our promise."

Meanwhile, Faralahy Mahery knew the time when the girl was born and when the time had come for her to be old enough to marry. So he came to get her to be his wife. He said, "I'm Faralahy Mahery. I know the girl is older now, so I'm coming to get her to be my wife and take her away."

"Yes," the girl's parents said, "but what name should we give her?"

"You should call her Isoamangitravelo," he said.[1]

But the girl said, "I am still young, and I don't feel I can leave my parents."

"If you can't leave your parents yet, then I will go my way again and come back when you are older." And he left.

When Isoamangitravelo grew older and older, she said to her parents, "Now I'm going to follow my husband because I am older and I can leave you." But she had no idea where he'd gone.

Her parents said, "If you leave, how will you be able to find him since you don't even know where he is now?"

"I'll leave, all the same, so bless me," she said.

When the blessing was done, Isoamangitravelo left her parents to follow Faralahy Mahery. Every time she saw a village, she called, singing:

Faralahy Mahery, Isoamangitravelo's husband.
Faralahy Mahery, Isoamangitravelo's husband.
He had been flapped away by the waves
    and reached Ambodivinany.[2]
I don't know if he's dead somewhere.
I don't know if he's alive somewhere.

"Keep going ahead, my dear,"[3] said those who answered her call. So Isoamangitravelo kept traveling to find another village, and she sang the same song to find Faralahy Mahery.

---

[1] *Isoamangitravelo* translates as "a beautiful young girl who smells of flowers."

[2] *Ambodivinany* contains *Ambody* which means "down," *vinany* meaning the confluence of two rivers—an estuary at a lake or at the sea.

[3] *Endriko* is translated as "my dear" but the literal meaning is "my mother," and the word is often used in the Southeast as an appellation for a cherished daughter or a sister, aunt, or other dear women.

A week had been passed. She reached a new village. Again she sang:

Faralahy Mahery, Isoamangitravelo's husband
Faralahy Mahery, Isoamangitravelo's husband.
He had been flapped away by the waves
    and reached Ambodivinany.
I don't know if he's dead somewhere.
I don't know if he's alive somewhere.

A man answered, "Faralahy Mahery is not here. That's why we can't see him, but I can replace him, so come up[4] here."

Once she came up to the village, he said to her, "Why are you still looking for Faralahy Mahery? I am also Faralahy Mahery. He is not worthy of you if he didn't come to fetch you to your parents' house, so I'm not going to let you go. You will become my wife now." And Isoamangitravelo became the man's wife.

Meanwhile, the right Faralahy Mahery arrived to the village of Isoamangitravelo's parents, but they said to him, "She left us to follow you."

Faralahy Mahery said to his parents-in-law, "Bless me so that I can find her." Then he left, and as he traveled, he sang the same song to find her:

I'm Faralahy Mahery, Isoamangitravelo's husband.
I'm Faralahy Mahery, Isoamangitravelo's husband.
She had been flapped away by the waves
    and reached Ambodivinany.
I don't know if she's dead somewhere.
I don't know if she's alive somewhere.

"Keep going ahead, Iabako,"[5] said those who answered the call. He kept going and each time he saw a village, he sang that song. Finally,

---

[4] "Come up": Villages used to be protected by a wall often made of a mixture of clay mud and eggs, and the village itself used to be settled in the heart of a mountain or a hill.

he came to a new village and he sang again, but now, Isoamangitravelo could hear him and answered his call:

I'm Isoamangitravelo, Faralahy Mahery's wife.
Can't be caught any more,
What's in the hand of the hawk.
Can't be caught any more,
What's in the hand of a man.

"Well," Faralahy Mahery said, "can't be caught any more, because she's in the hand of a man? I'm not resigned and I won't settle for that. We're going to fight," he said. But the people in the village said, "You can't have her back any more because she's already ours." And they threw spears, axes, and spades at him. But Faralahy Mahery managed to throw back what they had thrown at him. And in the end, no one could stay in the village except Isoamangitravelo, his wife.

That is why an Antaimoro woman can't go and find, or follow, her man, unless the man comes to get her to be his wife. The women do this because once they were misled by men.

—as told by Mme. Alphonsisme
(Fianarantsoa)

ഗ്രൂഗ്രൂഗ്രൂഗ്രൂഗ്രൂ

Ravolamamba and Tsaramiamby

Once upon a time, there was a young woman whose name was Ravola-mamba. She was a beautiful young woman and the daughter of the king. And there was Tsaramiamby, who was a son of a very wealthy

---

[5] *Iabako*: similar to the translation "my dear," but the literal meaning is "my father," and the word is often used in the Southeast as an appelation for a cherished man who is a son, a husband, an uncle, or any other man considered as a dear person.

family. Although his family was very wealthy, he didn't have any wife. So one day, Tsaramiamby told his father, "Father, I'll go far away to seek for something."

His father answered, "You want to go far away to seek something? What are you going to look for? If you look for money, you get some; if you look for fortune, we are wealthy enough; if you look for cattle, we have many of them. So what are you looking for?"

Tsaramiamby replied, "I want to dig the earth (meaning: looking for money, a job or a wife)."

"Dig the earth?" his father asked.

"Yes," he answered. Then he left his house and parents to dig the earth. When he walked out of the village where his parents lived, he found a cave where a fierce animal lived. He took off his fine cloth, and buried it in the cave.

"What are you doing here?" the animal demanded. "This village is ours and this place is ours."

"I am going to dig the earth."

"You're going to dig the earth? What kind of earth do you like to dig?"

"The kind where I can find my fortune. Although I have it with my parents: rice, we have it; cattle, we have them; but wife, I don't have. So that is the one I'm looking for."

"Then you can leave your fabric here," the animal said, "but remember that if you leave your fabric here and if, one day, you'll find a wife and you'll have children, we'll take your first child away. Do you agree?" the animal asked. "Yes, I do," Tsaramiamby answered. So he buried his fine cloth in the cave and he wrapped a gunnysack around himself like *sadika* (another kind of material which men wore around their waists, passing through the legs to cover the sex and the posterior).

When he arrived in a village, he asked the people, "Where is the king's palace?"

The people said, "Here," and they led him to the king's house. Once he came in the palace, he did not go to the corner where there were some seats; instead, he directly went to the corner where chickens were kept. The king, surprised, asked, "Why do you go directly to the corner where chickens are kept?"

"This is the place where I should be," Tsaramiamby said. "I come here to dig the earth."

"If you want to dig the earth," the king said, "I have some in the fields."

"It doesn't matter," Tsaramiamby said, "even if I have to feed your pigs." So the king made him do everything, including feeding his pigs. While feeding the pigs, he could see the king's daughter, Ravolamamba. And one day he told the king, "King, I think I like your daughter."

"You like my daughter?" the king said. Tsaramiamby told him that he did. So the king had a conversation with his daughter, Ravolamamba, but she refused and said, "Father, how could you give me someone as a husband who is digging in the fields, and who is only our servant and slave? Whatever happens, I'll refuse to get married with him."

So her father said, "Whatever happens on the earth or in the heaven, you'll get married with him even if he is just our servant or slave." And her mother, the queen, also consented.

Ravolamamba cried and cried all the time, because she didn't want to get married with Tsaramiamby. But she had to do as her father commanded. After living together for about a year, Tsaramiamby told his parents-in-law, "I must go back home and I will take my wife with me because I'm tired of working here."

"If you want to go home, you can take her with our consent," the king said. But Ravolamamba kept crying. Tsaramiamby, seeing that, was moved with compassion, and said, "If you don't like me, gather the people of the village and push aside an orange. The one who is pointed out by the orange will become your husband, if I'm not worthy of you."

So her parents gathered the village and made her do as Tsaramiamby told with her other sisters. When she pushed aside the orange, it went directly to Tsaramiamby. Ravolamamba was so disappointed that she started crying again. "Don't cry any more," Tsaramiamby said, "because I am your share if the orange came up to me. Let's go back home and I'll take you to the place where I live." He took her to his village.

When they arrived near the cavern where the animal lived, Tsaramiamby said, "I'm going to bathe."

"Are you going to bathe in that deep water where an animal lives?" Ravolamamba asked him.

"Yes, I am," he answered, "so keep walking." Ravolamamba stepped a little farther to wait for him. When he finished bathing, he dug up the fine cloth he formerly wore and that he had buried into the cave. He put it on and joined Ravolamamba. "Let's take our way again," he said.

But when she saw him, she was astounded and could not recognize him dressed as he was in a fine cloth. She said, "You are not my husband. His name is Tsaramiamby and he's still bathing."

"I am Tsaramiamby," he said. But Ravolamamba insisted that her husband was still bathing. "You don't tell me a lie because I'm not going to go with you." He tried to convince her again and said, "I am Tsaramiamby. Let's leave this place now."

Reluctantly, Ravolamamba went with him. And when they arrived in the village, she was surprised to see the hundred servants welcoming Tsaramiamby. She was so surprised that she asked, "Who among your relatives lives here?"

"The parents who gave me birth," he said.

"Then whose house is this?"

"Ours," he said.

"If you live here, what did you want to find when you worked for my father?"

"I was digging the earth, but we are so wealthy, that's why I covered myself with those shabby clothes and worked for your father. I wanted to find my fortune."

Ravolamamba said, "If it is so, I'll become your wife because you're someone who is very wealthy. Let's go back to my parents' village and do the marriage rituals, and tell them that I like you and want to get married with you."

When they arrived in the village where Ravolamamba's parents lived, she told them all about Tsaramiamby and their wish to get married. Then her parents gathered the people of the village to announce that Ravolamamba would become Tsaramiamby's wife.

The days, months, and years elapsed, and she got pregnant and finally had a baby boy. One day, the animal showed itself to Tsaramiamby through a dream. "The day has come," it said, "so I'll come to take my reward away."

But Tsaramiamby didn't want to leave the baby for the animal, so he didn't give the baby to it. Days and months elapsed, and the baby came up to the stage of crawling. When he was old enough, Ravolamamba made him sleep alone in another room. That night, while the baby slept, the animal took the baby away and they couldn't find the baby the next morning. Ravolamamba and Tsaramiamby were out of their minds seeking for the baby in vain.

But one day, there was an old man living in the neighborhood, who went searching for firewood. In the forest, he could hear the animal's voice soothing the baby and singing:

Don't cry Ravolamamba's son, don't cry!
Don't cry Tsaramiamby's son, don't cry!
Good thing exchanged to good thing.
Beautiful thing exchanged to beautiful thing.
Don't cry, dear child!

The old man came back home immediately and told the village, "I was looking for firewood when I heard a voice soothing a baby near a cave I passed where a fierce animal lives. I heard that we are looking for a baby, so maybe Tsaramiamby's son is in this cave, but I do not dare to go there. You must send five men to listen to the voice first because when the baby cries, the voice sings:

Don't cry Ravolamamba's son, don't cry!
Don't cry Tsaramiamby's son, don't cry!
Good thing exchanged to good thing.
Beautiful thing exchanged to beautiful thing.
Don't cry, dear child!

So the five men were pointed out by the king to search this cave.
When they arrived by the place where the animal lived, they could
hear the voice soothing the baby again and sang:

Don't cry Ravolamamba's son, don't cry!
Don't cry Tsaramiamby's son, don't cry!
Good thing exchanged to good thing.
Beautiful thing exchanged to beautiful thing.
Don't cry, dear child!

Perplexed, the five men said to each other, "How can we get the baby
out of the cave since none of us is able to go down there?" The king
decreed that the one who could get the baby out of the cave would be
offered seven head of cattle. The five men came back to the village and
reported that it was not possible to get the baby out.

But there was a man who was called Faralahy Mahery (the strong,
youngest son), and he said: "Let me get the baby out. I feel able to
do it."

So the people of the village surrounded the cave and Faralahy Mahery stepped stealthily into the darkness. When he arrived, he stroked
the water that flowed underground with a rod. The animal was startled
and ran away, leaving the baby behind. Faralahy Mahery took the baby
out of the cave, and the king gave him the seven head of cattle and invited the whole village to a big feast. When the feast was over, the king
said to his people, "From now on, none of you is allowed to make a baby
sleep alone in a separate room."

And that is why the Antaimoro's ancestors, even nowadays, tell the people not to let a baby sleep alone in a separate room since the baby will be taken away by something in the night, and never found again.

—as told by Mme. Alphonsisme
(Fianarantsoa)

CHAPTER VI

PEOPLE OF THE HIGHLANDS;
PEOPLE OF THE LONG VALLEYS;
PEOPLE OF THE THORNS

Lamba tohy tsy an'olon-jejo, lamba lava tsy an'olon-kamo.
The well-wrapped lamba does not belong to the wanton,
nor does the long lamba to the lazy.

On Sunday afternoons, in meeting places on the outskirts of Tana, people come from all over the country to listen to *hiragasy*, the song-poems of Madagascar. They meet in churches, school auditoriums, dance halls, and cattle auction rooms. They come from districts throughout the capital city, and from surrounding villages—old and young, male and female, city and village folks.

I was recovering from a fever the first time I attended a Sunday *hiragasy*. I had worried that I would succumb to the medication I was taking, but once I was inside, sitting on one of the hard benches in a school auditorium, the lingering traces of my illness vanished as I watched the performance of singers and musicians wearing the colors of their districts—their coats and dresses piped in contrasting colors—red for the soil of Madagascar and sunsets that ignite the sky, and blue for the endless sky and for the ocean that surrounds the land of the ancestors. I was caught up in another fever, applauding with the crowd to songs of love and death, wealth and pride, war and poverty, families and enemies, wisdom and foolishness, all echoing in the rafters with the drumbeat and trumpet blasts of the musicians.

Inset map shows location of Antananarivo (big star), Ivato, Antsirabe,
and Fianarantsoa

Hira, to sing. *Gasy*, of the Malagasy people. I could find no definition for
hiragasy in the few Malagasy–English dictionaries that were available.
In those dictionaries, *hira* was defined simply as singing, but there was
no reference to the special songs of *hiragasy*. I surmised that the songs of
the people must have been too dangerously close to notions of sedition for
the colonialists and missionaries who first constructed those dictionaries.
Perhaps they were right to be worried. There was certainly the beauty of
independence in the songs, a sense that the singers had tapped into a great
treasury of Malagasy spirit and determination through *hainteny* (poems),
ohabolana (proverbs), and *angano* (stories). The song-poems were woven
into a tapestry of oral traditions—traditions that had lived on despite attempts during colonial rule to suppress them.

Song-poems of *hiragasy* were steeped in the history and culture of the
Malagasy people, but the costumes reflected colonial intrusion, albeit
tempered with Malagasy flair. They worked in teams, each group consisting of ten or twelve singers, more or less evenly divided between
men and women; and there were three or four musicians playing
percussion, reed, and stringed instruments. The men wore fedoras and
frock coats, their lambas draped in the manner of bandoliers. Watching
the men, I could easily recall the New Orleans Preservation Blues Bands
I'd seen marching in Mardi Gras parades, or thirty-second degree
Masons in their black suits and white bandoliers on parade in New York,
St. Louis, or Atlanta. In one *hiragasy* group, a young boy danced on one
leg for what seemed like twenty minutes. He crossed and recrossed the
leg he kept off the ground, his gestures acknowledging the presence of
the ancestors, the *vitana* or destiny of the people. It was a dance that
could only be performed by someone who was youthful, who was able
to make difficult movements seem easy. In another group, the orator,
whose duty it was to call forth the songs, was over six feet tall, a long-
limbed man with pronounced cheekbones and a determined jaw. (I
would not see another Malagasy that tall until I met the poet M. Rado.)
The orator had a commanding presence, his words resounding throughout the auditorium when he began the performance by placing his gray

fedora on the drum to show respect for the ancestors before he called upon their guidance.

Traditionally, *hiragasy* was used to entertain kings and visiting royalty, but the song-poems also were steeped in village history, and carried into the twentieth century by the Malagasy insistence on paying homage to the ancestors. At the beginning of each performance, the ancestors were called upon. "Please help us," the orator beseeched. "We are poor and not wise as you. We are still here among the living." While he spoke, everyone took their positions—men, women, men, women—as if they were at a cotillion. The women singers wore floor length dresses, more early nineteenth century than twentieth: short puff sleeves, high necks, abbreviated lambas worn as scarves. Their voices held the high, lilting quality of choral singers.

Throughout the country, I repeatedly saw the link between music and the oral tradition. Wherever Tiana and I visited storytellers, we also found musicians. In Toliara, we had watched a performance of M. Manindry's dance troupe before listening to the storyteller, M. Soaraza. In Fianarantsoa, we listened to street musicians play the wonderful melodies of the *jejy voatavo* before returning to Mme. Alphonsisme's house to listen to her stories under the blanket of a starry sky. Sometimes a visit yielded only music. Such was the case in Ambondrona and Ambalatoratasy, two small villages near Fianarantsoa.

Simon had taken us into the hills to find a storyteller, but instead we found several villages recovering from the effects of malaria. These were tiny farming communities nestled in hillsides where there were more rocks than trees, and unmarked roads were, often as not, impassable. In Ambalatoratasy, where several people had been taken ill from the disease, I met Efraim Romaine, who was about nine years old and the youngest storyteller I encountered. He had been out of bed for only a few days after battling malaria, and remembering how a month earlier I'd battled an infection, I suggested he needed to rest. But he shyly tried to piece together a tale he'd been told by his grandmother. Although his

Chatting with village boys framed in a car window, Ambalatoratasy

efforts yielded only fragments of the story, I still saw clear promise of his
beginnings as an orator. The older boys of the village fared only a little
better with their handmade guitars and drums, but everyone joined in,
including Efraim's family, all of them dancing and applauding the young
musicians.

Later, we continued up the gravel road toward Ambondrona. In a village nearby, we learned that the community was preparing for a funeral.
Malaria had taken its toll in the area with eight people dead, including
three children. I waited in the car while Tiana went with Simon and
Haingo to learn where the funeral would be held. While I waited, two
young boys, curious about a private car so near their homes, chatted with
me through the window, our language consisting mostly of gestures and
laughter but communication all the same. As we drove closer to Ambondrona, the signs of funeral preparation were more apparent. We saw a

group of a dozen or so choral singers making their way to the ceremony. They had time to spare, they told us, and stopped long enough to take us back to the elder's house for a private recital of *sarandra* and song-poems of the countryside that was their home. Everyone within hailing distance crowded into the small room, the adults making space in front for the children. And everyone gave the group their rapt attention, urging them on to favorite songs—the children delighted with the songs of *arira*, the fables of animals, and the singers showing their choral skills with increasingly difficult pieces. "They may go to the city to participate in a *hiragasy*," Tiana said, "so every day, they take the time to practice." I knew that group would go with the support of all who lived in Ambondrona. There was a sense of family and place, a sense of belonging—both because everyone knew the singers and because they knew every song. And when we entered the village where everyone was gathering for the funeral, the elders and orators were singing some of those same songs.

The songs of *hiragasy* were a shared part of Malagasy culture, some repeated so often that every schoolchild in Madagascar knew the words. The most popular were those that spoke of romantic love and those that captured *tantara*, tales of history and legend told in reverential verse. Some songs were sad tributes to lost children, those who have strayed into the modern world and turned their backs on tradition; some songs were bawdy reminders to lovers to remain true to one another. Some were songs of poetic dispute—the men offering their version of the story, the women countering with their version, the audience cheering them on to more elaborate retorts. And elaborate they were. Like other forms of the oral traditions of Madagascar, the *hiragasy* were rich in metaphor and symmetry, allusion and association, rhyme and temporal accents of the Malagasy language, all of which was strengthened by the musical accompaniment of trumpets, violins, and drums. When I marveled at how spontaneous the songs appeared to be, Tiana said, "These groups practice many years, but they must not look practiced."

She was right. Each performance was certainly more than just memory. The singers also needed to possess that sense of history and culture which set them, and their people, apart from the rest of the world. Perhaps that was another reason why the missionaries had not included *hiragasy* in dictionaries of translation. It was as if the very act of *hiragasy* reflected the metaphorical nature of the language and the culture, a state where the literal meaning seemed as obvious as the ease in which the song was performed—but in reality, every line held a metaphorical underpinning, a balance of life, breath, and strength. The veil of easy answers had to be raised in order to understand the true meaning of a phrase. These songs were lyrical poems, the strength of the verse pulled from the lives of the people who continued to celebrate the songs.

ぬぬぬぬぬ

It Was There But Goes By Quickly

Orator's Admonishment:

He set out at the break of day to look for money but it could not be found because it is difficult to look for money when the little that comes in does not stay but goes to Mahajanga.

Others work in the office every day.

My dear elder brother: watch your step, for life is a hardship, because duty is unfulfilled when it is abandoned for money. Sickness is not healed without money. If one dies, penniless, he will be buried in the ground.[1] We are doomed to inherit Death.

---

[1] Malagasy saying: It is only a poor man who cannot be buried in a tomb but must be buried in the ground.

The rich must die; those with trunkfuls of money must die; when destiny arrives, you die. What can be done, what is the solution to defeat Death?

If Death can be bought, only the poor will fill the grave. Wealthy people find peace. My dear friends, consider how life ends quickly. Beautiful hair has to be given up there in the grave. Good physiques have to be given up there in the grave. Relatives can never be seen again. It's up to you not to love your relatives. It's up to you not to have so much jealousy. Heaven does not belong to spiteful people.

You must explore in order to find money; whether it is hard or easy, you cannot be consoled. Exhaust yourself to get something; but frequently, it is astounding: the little that comes does not stay but is empty.

Running there to Mahajanga;[2] you skip to Toliara; running to Maintirano, in this place that is not worth mentioning. But frequently, it is astounding: the little that comes does not stay but is empty.

There are others who work in an office; there are some others who do a simple job every day. There are some others who raise animals or farm the land. But frequently, it is astounding: the little that comes does not stay but is empty.

Then let's peel away the story. All of you must listen carefully. You are the listeners but we are the tellers. Don't agree if it doesn't seem clear. For this is neither a fable nor a legend but advice to be given in a song. You people, we beg you to listen: when there are not words enough, then we will complete it together.

---

[2] Mahajanga: to be in the city rather than a poor man in the country.

Father sets out at daybreak to seek, to search for this money. With no thought of fatigue, mother works hard (remember) to seek this wealth. But the little that comes does not stay but seems to pass by. Whether too much or too little, it does not stay but is used up and gone.

It was there but passed by quickly . . .

Money is difficult to find but it seems to be astounding when it comes there inside the household only to flee and not settle happily. Locked inside a trunk but still it flees. Kept in an armoire but still it seems to run away. It was there but passed by rapidly.

Secondly, examine closely the clothing. Disregard the money and wealth wrapped over ourselves and worn. Thirdly, examine, if you will, this life. Little may not be expected to change while you are young. Days and nights move stealthily, but soon turn over and change in a minute.

It was there but passed by rapidly . . .

Really, the eyewitness will examine carefully the car. Examine carefully the long road where the car is not sufficient for rapid passage. You may expect the car to be reliable because it has a motor. The car vibrates along the road for a few years, then dies.

It was there but passed by rapidly . . .

That's not all, dear Father. Listen. There is still something we'd like to say. Let's talk about money for a style of living: mankind is not dry but wet.[3] What you don't have gives you great suffering.

---

[3] Malagasy saying: To be wet is to look for a better life. To be dry is to be slothful.

You must explore in order to find money, whether it is hard or easy, you cannot be consoled. Exhaust yourself to get something but frequently, it is astounding: the little that comes does not stay but is empty.

Running there to Mahajanga; you skip to Toliara; running to Maintirano, in this place that is not worth mentioning. But frequently, it is astounding: the little that comes does not stay but is empty.

There are others who work in an office; there are some others who do a simple job every day. There are some others who raise animals or farm the land. But frequently, it is astounding: the little that comes does not stay but is empty.

My dear young brother, take care with what you buy before bargaining or you will be ashamed to find only pennies, only lint in your pockets. Since when you have only small provisions for the journey, this is unbearable indeed because when you are exhausted, you don't have anything to bargain with; so you end up unable to avoid rolling over in the dirt, having lost your mat of palm fronds. That, indeed I say, is what makes me tell this: each of us makes an effort, then always courageous seeks a better life; Death is unavoidable and arrives when money is not there, when you cannot avoid falling in a hole in the ground.

The *hiragasy* is our main reason for being here. May it never be, God forbid, that we give you false directions. Is that true or not: you do not seem to say anything or are you amazed by this?

—as heard in Antananarivo
Sunday *Hiragasy*

Like the song-poems of *hiragasy*, Malagasy poetry, the verse form called *hainteny*, flourishes in the ornamentation of language. As a poet, I did not find that surprising. Poets the world over are enamored with language,

with the rhythms, allusions, and cultural or metaphorical associations reflected in the poem. The poem details both the history and the pride of
the people—in a word, its nationhood. So it is no coincidence that poets
are often among the first revolutionaries, and among the first to be per-
secuted. In Madagascar, the life of the poet was altered considerably by
the presence of missionaries and colonialists. It is said that Ranavalona I,
the Merina queen, imposed a sanction on transcribing the oral traditions
of the Malagasy people for fear that there would be an attempt by missionaries "to change the customs of my ancestors." But members of her
court had already begun writing down *hainteny*. The scribes, educated in
missionary schools, had initiated the shift of *hainteny* from strictly oral to
written forms; however, it wasn't until the twentieth century that French
translators began to recognize the poetic forms of *hainteny*. That recognition was a double-edged sword. During the French occupation, it had
been dangerous to be a poet. "To be a scholar of any sort was dangerous,"
Tiana said. Malagasy poets were jailed, or exiled, and Malagasy students
read French poets. "We read some poems of Jean-Joseph Rabearivelo but
not many," she said.

Jean-Joseph Rabearivelo and his predecessor, Ramanantoanina, are in-
disputably the grandfathers of Malagasy poetry in its written form. Although Ramanantoanina, who died in 1940 at the age of forty-nine, was
translated into French, he wrote his poems in Malagasy, enabling the
metaphorical associations, as Queen Ranavalona had ordered, to hide the
secrets of Malagasy folklore from translators who were unfamiliar with
the history and culture of the country. Ramanantoanina was exiled for
his defiance of French rule; and as a result, the focus of some of his poems was diaspora, the melancholy of *hanina* and *embona*, that longing for
place when one is separated from the beloved homeland. Ramanantoanina continued to be saddened by his country's oppression, to write poems
inspired by the *tanindrazana*, "the ground of the ancestors." A similar
sense of despair also followed Jean-Joseph Rabearivelo, who was thirty-
six when he committed suicide in 1937. His poems are exquisitely crafted,

a blend of traditional *hainteny* and contemporary patterns, and have earned him international recognition. Rabearivelo's poetry reveals a great passion for language, particularly for the elusive quality of proverbs and riddles that symbolize the cultural context of poetic associations. In his poems, the unmentionable, that which is taboo, is explored. This is true for contemporary Malagasy poets as well. The poems of Flavian Ranaivo, an expatriate living in France, are profoundly influenced by *hainteny*. For many, the *hainteny* allows them to both conceal and reveal, to employ those traditional metaphorical devices that became the sustaining features of Malagasy poetry during the colonial period.

"Many poets decided not to write poems during the revolution," Mme. Madeline told me. She was a young woman during the bloody 1947 rebellion when one-third of the population of Madagascar had been killed in the uprising. "We tried to write poems, but when the French began to arrest us, I burned all that I had written." Though I didn't realize it at the time, Mme. Madeline would not be the only Malagasy poet I would meet who had resorted to destroying poems rather than have them confiscated by the French. It was as if Queen Ranavalona's dictum was still being observed.

"I did not write for years," Mme. Madeline said, "but now I write about love."

Her poems were about more than courtship and marriage; they expressed a love of country, and of the seasons that depleted and nourished it. It was raining in Antsirabe the day I met Mme. Madeline. The windows in the parlor of the Manoro Hotel were streaked with moisture. After a week of falling asleep to the sound of rain arriving on schedule at night, the downpour had taken us by surprise that morning. The garden was soggy with rain, flowers drooping under the weight, and the light was full of green shadows.

"This is the season when we are blessed with rain," Mme. Madeline said.

"I know this kind of weather," I replied, and told her about the rain forests of the Pacific Northwest.

We talked about the sound of rain, something so simple, so natural, "but it's a part of life," she said. She told me that most of her poems were about love and family, "also a part of life." She talked about her poem "Water: The Source of Life"—a simple verse, she called it. But I noticed that the second part of the title included the phrase "Not New But Timeless," indicating the cycles of life and death. Her lyricism reminded me of early *hainteny* verse, where images of nature were eloquently woven into the *ohabolana*, the proverbial framework of the poem. This lyricism is evident in her poem "Moonlight":

७⌇ ७⌇ ७⌇ ७⌇ ७⌇

Moonlight

1.

Moon in the sky
Shining luminescent and quiet
Look down and bring joy to our land
It has been said you always change
We don't know but that is what we think
Today you seem delighted
Tomorrow you will grow cold
So strange that we cannot determine
If it is a riddle or just a rumor
It is so obvious that it is not easy to tell

2.

It is moonlight
Shining like the sun

Sparkling glimmering bright
A distant echo of songs and applause
And children delighted and radiant
And those lovers able to enjoy precious moments
Under the glance of the lonely moon
Those lovers know they have taken the right road

3.

That distant moon rising slowly from the ocean floor
The moonlight, my dear friends, shimmers like gold
Like a precious jewel we cannot afford
We have to give up the brilliant sky rejoicing
The moon rises higher and higher
Admire the multitude of stars welcoming
The rising moon as if to say
Let us surround the moon

4.

When the moon grows dark in eclipse
Wait and never lose courage
Life is like the moon
No need to complain
Today you are famished
Tomorrow you will be satisfied
Life is like hide-and-seek
You cannot sneak a look my dear friends
The moon is overcast and suddenly life's misery
Disappears as the moon reappears

—Mme. Madeline
(Antsirabe)

ᑩᑩᑩᑩᑩ

Water: The Source of Life
Old-fashioned Medicine, Not New But Timeless

1.
There is a beautiful thing I will tell you
    Indeed you do not expect only a new thing
        Not wind or fire, but one tremendous force
            When there is not enough to drink, the skin seems ashen

2.
Once upon a time they say, there were flood waters
    God changed his mind. There will never again be this disaster
        Next time, He says, I will use it to do good
            To prove this, I will show you a rainbow

3.
Many years until now, life went smoothly
    Occasionally there was no water. A complaint could be heard
        "Then what will we eat, how will we wash clothes, bathe?"
            Occasionally when days were scorching hot, you grew tired

4.
Whatever we do here on this earth
    Even if joy appears or even if sorrow happens
        Use always this gift of God's
            As soon as it passes upon the earth, hunger's destroyed

5.
Once the people are born, or they die
    They are bathed clean to deserve the Almighty

Still that water just washes the soul
Family baptism or Christian baptism, names do not matter

6.
You may water the flowers, then see them radiantly bloom
It is easy to find this remedy for those who are unhappy
Our clothes become pure and clean and dirt has floated away
When you are tired, a bath will ease your load

7.
Please, think about that when you see the tick birds bathing
Happily flapping their wings. Singing, so to speak
As do ducks and geese. Everyone knows this.
When it rains, they are so wet, they seem to swim in a river

8.
Still there is a bad side. Occasionally there are floods
It's necessary for the living to flee, not to yell: STOP
But a good thing the water hides, not to be bartered or sold
It brings the breath of life, a cheap gift

9.
A very good remedy but too easy a price
Cirrhosis or bile or the heart's need to beat with wild anger
Take advantage of dear life because it is given by God
Simply this: cold water. That is what we call it

10.
Have you ever tried what we call the healing waters?
It cleans our insides. An easy remedy, drink some
When you awake in the morning, during the day, or at bedtime
Drink some regularly, every day and your vexation leaves

11.

Try and you will feel a great change
  You will feel fulfilled, I'll bet you
    It is an amazing medicine, I declare
      Not new, but here since ancient times

                —Mme. Madeline
                (Antsirabe)

The poet Ernest Rakotosalama was also a product of the revolution. When we arrived at his house in Fianarantsoa, I was somewhat out of breath and distracted. His house was near the top of one of Fianar's circular streets, a cobblestone hill climb of stairsteps, impassable by car. Simon had dropped Tiana and me at the foot of the intersecting street, and by the time we'd climbed the sixty or so steps, I was winded. We had arrived in late evening, when the shadows were beginning to turn a dull red in the fading sunlight. As we moved up the hill, away from the city traffic, the air seemed thinner, cooler after the heat of the day. There were small courtyards in the crook of each set of stairs where children took advantage of the last of the light to play one more game. That was what had distracted me—the familiar chants of games as dusk hastened the children home.

I have to confess that I was reluctant to move away from the sounds of children and walk into M. Ernest's flat; their playful rhymes reminded me of games I'd played in the summer afternoons of my childhood. But the children's voices quickly faded as soon as I stepped in the door. In the single light of the small, one room apartment, there were stacks of books, boxes of them haphazardly placed on the floor and a few shelves along the walls. The books seemed old, fragile, the paper turning brown with age. M. Ernest offered me a seat, removing books from the cushion of a chair. I read one title—an early French edition of Malagasy poetry. When I brushed my fingers against it, I was afraid it would fall apart. Papers were stacked in boxes in the corners, at the foot of the bed, on the

Poet, Ernest Rakotosamala, Fianarantsoa

table that also served as his eating space. What I remember most about him was his intense eyes, large and watery brown, inspecting me in the shadowy light. Was he trying to see if I was uncomfortable? "Many people have come to see him, to take pictures and to ask about poems," Tiana had warned before we'd arrived. "He may not be interested in giving you some poems."

I smiled, admired the books he had, and commented that he must be well read. His eyes never shifted from my face, but he began to talk, slowly at first, then more animated when he saw that I was truly interested in his collection of books. "Only recently has it been possible to keep so many books," Tiana translated. "Now he has a daughter who lives in America. But he also gets books from France."

He told us how difficult it had been to own books during the colonial years. "Malagasy students," he said, "could not sit for the university exams, and many were arrested. When I heard they might arrest me, I quickly came home and burned my poems."

I told him that I'd met other Malagasy poets who spoke of the years of revolution, and the struggle toward an independence that had been hard won. He said that in those years, he'd write poems, memorize them, then destroy the written copy. We talked about how poetry could be a thread to the past—to honor the ancestors or recall oppression. "There are many stories, many poems," he said. "You must learn to listen. To make words sing."

"He tells us that with the ancestors, he knows how to listen," Tiana translated. "The poem can speak what they hear."

M. Ernest spoke passionately about what makes the Malagasy poet distinct from other poets: from the *fitenin-drazana*—advice given by the ancestors—to the lamba, the rice fields, and the red earth of Madagascar. "They are separate but always related," he said. "So when we speak of life and death, we speak of these things."

"Like the songs of *hiragasy*," I said. "They also speak of life and death."

He turned his patient eyes upon me. "It is the Malagasy spirit," he said.

༺༻༺༻༺༻

The Way to Say Farewell

I.
The birds no longer fly
The cattle never stop bellowing

The honey never loses its sweet taste
The sun is no longer in the sky
The crossroads separate the path
Those who have gone before own this path
At day's end you close the door

    The speech in the brain never stops
    The talking never smells bad
    Our conversation is so sweet
    Because there is no residue like honey
    Not crunchy like salt
    Not scratchy like sugar cane
    For it is equal to swallowing a tiny crab
    Pleasing like honey in the milk:
    And sweetly fragrant

The red sun makes you long for home
For we are shared by distant gardens
The hills are distant from the valley
The waterfall is swallowed by the river
The house is divided by rooms
And so we leave you even if we are unwilling
We must separate although we are reluctant
Then the slightest goodbyes that we will say
We leave you with the chosen farewell
Because this happiness is something aside
And does not keep me from longing for home

    The sun has almost set
    And we will hurry home
    For night hurries us
    The night is not white
    And we have no torch

If by chance we encounter the snake with a large mouth
So instead of washing, we are dirty

And so goodbye, they say, good people
Have a long life, kind father
We will meet another day
The beautiful morning comes quickly
The toothache doesn't come suddenly
And so a great transplanting of rice must come
Our farewell is not like that of the whistling teal ruffling its feathers
Our farewell is not the farewell of the passerby who only shakes his
    lamba and leaves
Our farewell will not make our goodbye the farewell of fire which
    leaves ashes
Our farewell will be the farewell of burnt rice which gives golden red
    color to rice water
Our farewell is not the farewell of summer that ends with thunder
    and hail
But the farewell of winter that will shake off dry leaves
That grow into green shoots in the spring
Our farewell is not the farewell of fog that separates us forever
But the farewell of the sun that makes us meet again in the morning
Ours is the farewell of love, the farewell of those unwilling to part
And so after shaking hands, kissing hands will make us long for each .
    other

  Yes, dear people, be well when we part
  Be good when we won't be meeting
  In order to have a wonderful talk the next time
  When we are caught in the circle of day and night
  And so arrive well the way you have passed
  We will not go the way of the waterfall
  Go ahead and never go back

Here you keep the village
Even though we have gone
Again we will come back another day

Farewell Farewell to those who belong to the same village
End well the night to awaken well
Farewell my friends: while we do not meet
Farewell of lovers and kiss and embrace

II.

Even if the market is closed
Pot sellers never leave
Even if the water in the river is dried up
The sand still waits there

Danger and misfortune are not begged to return
But even if you have gone, come back frequently
Don't let us miss you as we daydream
So that poor health is insulted by the summer
The heart does not limp, so pass by frequently
The eye looking at a distance doesn't get strained
Make someone come to the gate of the village
Don't let the way to come here get worn out

We are clay jugs not used to fetch water
Whether far and near the place where we are
You come either day or night
The gate will be opened when you visit
We bless you in that far-off place
In order to be well to go there; in order to be well to return
If we must choose: Let us stay here
Since the flood waters are angry when they meet
Only ugly toads go together

The chickens shake off their chicks that peck each other
The pinch without the fight is another pleasure
But tied together in memory
Leave messages when someone passes by
But when it is cloudy there, it is partly cloudy on this side
When blossoming there, here the flowers bud

  The people going home are followed until they are out of sight
  The heart on the other hand is with you always
  Although the handshakes were not tied
  Although these messages were stopped
  Because the sun has almost set
  We won't blame you if you go
  But may bless with water where you arrive

And so the place where you go is very very far
The different village will not allow us to be together
We do not drive you away but you really want to go home
So we do not blame you if you want to return to your nest
You left, we still remain here
The tree trunk invites the birds to come
May heaven grant your wish
Give you long days and golden moments
Make us meet for a lively talk again

  May you be better so danger will fall away from you
  But you will be sweet to be loved by what is good
  Your children will fill the village
  Your cattle pen will never be empty
  They will grow in the stable and bellow every day
  May your rice fields not be empty at springtime
  You won't regret it if you have to throw stones at the rice sparrow
  The rice in the granary will last throughout the year

The food you cook will be plentiful and not watered down
But in the morning when you soak the burnt rice, may it move
May the smoke of many cooking fires never leave your roof
Your family will never know a white night

You will leave and say goodbye
We here offer farewell
Put your farewell in your lamba
To make you beautiful when you go to the ceremony
To warm you on a winter's day
And it will be a means to wave to each other when we meet

Goodbye, goodbye, not to forget each other
Goodbye, goodbye, to remember each other
Be good to use the plant and not be sick
To make you healthy there
Goodbye, goodbye, they say not forever
Stay alive to meet again
Yes, you have gone but not to die
But your wooden door will be opened in the morning
The door will be closed in the evening
Sleep without nightmares
You will hear the rooster announcing the day
You will find the sun always shining

We say farewell and follow with a proper goodbye
Followed by a wish not to be spilled on the ground
Not to fail to get the destiny that is in front of you
But to be alive all along, with the good piled up like stairs
You will meet an abundance of good and what is delicious
May the breath of the earth make fragrant your life
May the blessing come from heaven above to bring you success
And so goodbye, goodbye indeed

Just farewell, into sleep or stumble
That all thus ends sweetly

PROVERBS:

If you cook a stone in water, the water will be cooked but not the stone.

To spend a white night is to go to bed hungry.

—Ernest Rakotosamala
(Fianarantsoa)

I suspect I was still thinking of the traditional forms of poetry and song found in *hiragasy* when I set out to meet Georges Andriamanantena, the poet known as Rado, at his house in Ivato, near Tana. Aside from Leonard Fox's 1990 publication of English translations of *hainteny*, traditional Malagasy verse forms, my whole sense of the poetry of the country had been based on translations of the poets Flavien Ranaivo and Jean-Joseph Rabearivelo. Their poems capture the musical patterns of Malagasy language and the rhythmical patterns of its verse in the same way that the poems of Yeats and Keats epitomize the classic traditions of English verse. Although my recent introduction to the oral traditions of *hiragasy* song-poems had begun to change my views, I was still inclined to think of Malagasy poetry as somewhat ritualized exaltations of the land and the ancestors, verse forms that were more elaborate than proverbs but certainly pastoral in nature. M. Rado would be my first encounter with a modern poet, one who dealt with contemporary themes and whose sense of home had sharpened his world view.

As soon as I stepped out of the taxi in front of his house, I felt as if I were entering a world of shared cultures. I was struck first by the architecture of the house, its lines so clearly Asian, I was transported, for a moment, back to Ipoh, Malaysia, or the suburbs of Kyoto, Japan. The house was a low-roofed bungalow with windows designed like shoji

With Georges Andriamanantena, the poet known as Rado, and his wife, in Ivato

screens, panels of translucent glass crosshatched with thin strips of wood. We sat in a wood paneled room, sipping cups of fragrant tea. With the windows open, the garden seemed to be a part of the room, the scent of flowers and songs of calling birds punctuating our conversation.

M. Rado was over six feet tall, graying at the temples, his angular features lending him a distinguished look. His wife reminded me of Gwendolyn Knight, a sculptor and the wife of African American painter Jacob Lawrence. Like Ms. Knight, Mme. Andriamanantena had the kind of beauty that some women keep well at any age. Under a crown of gray hair, her face was unlined and her smile radiant. She was at ease talking about her husband's work and their life together.

Before the revolution, before the French were finally expelled from

Madagascar, M. Rado had been jailed many times. "The French did not want us to sit for university exams, to write poems, to speak with pride about our country," he said. "We were told that we were French. But I did not go to jail for being French."

We talked about the conscious need for political poetry, from my standpoint as an African American poet who understood all too well the issues of racism in the Western World, and from his perspective as a Malagasy poet who had weathered cultural imperialism. Some of M. Rado's poems were lyrical, reminiscent of the metaphors and symbols found in traditional *ohabolana*, or proverbs, but others were more direct. He explained how his poems often used the traditional *hainteny* forms to address contemporary issues, but in others he leaned toward the style of contemporary free verse. One, "*Isan'andro Vaky Izao*," written in the sixties, was a protest of the Vietnam War. Tiana said, "He was to go to America, but because of that poem, the Americans would not give him permission. It was too dangerous." We laughed at the irony of the "free world" suppressing a poet who had experienced colonial oppression. "In poetry," he said, "the heart is filled." I listened to his poems while the room grew fragrant with the smell of jasmine tea and freshly baked vanilla cookies that his wife had prepared, and indeed my heart was filled. That is the wonder of poetic language—to hear the beauty of its music and know the strength of its images. And in the bright sunlight of that afternoon, the scent of flowers wafting in from the garden, I sometimes did not need to have Tiana translate for me.

Before we left, M. Rado asked if he could get a ride to the main road. "I must buy some things for dinner," he said. We took him to the highway, a busy intersection where drivers, in typical Malagasy fashion, obeyed no speed limits except their own. That's how I remember M. Rado—a tall, angular figure standing by the side of the road, the dust from passing cars billowing around him. In the faint sunlight of early evening, he looked both strong and vulnerable. I wanted to say: Let's go back. We can't leave him out there, alone. But we sped toward Tana, and what I remember is his figure centered in the back window of Simon's car, swirls of red dust clouding the view. A month later, I read that M. Rado's daughter, her husband, and three children were killed in an auto accident by a drunk driver on that highway. Television Madagascar ran footage of the funeral as the whole nation mourned along with him. "We treasure our poets," a poet from Tana said. "My students at the University read the works of many poets. Rabearivelo, Ramanantoanina, Ranaivo, Rado. They are a part of our past and our future."

පපපපප

Each Day Now Breaks

Because I implore
and beg you
to seek out
and gather names
to stop the war —
No joke, God forbid!

Somewhere in Vietnam,
each day now splits
the high ground and forest
the rice fields and stables
the valleys and hills
reeds and thrashing floors
all set ablaze, burned
in billowing smoke
like roiling volcanoes . . .
you can see it whirling
and filling all boundaries
to the very rim of the sky
the stench of gunpowder

drenching every place
as each day now breaks
Somewhere in Vietnam!

And so I entreat you
to sign
to petition,
No joking, may it never be,
No taunting because
Somewhere in Vietnam
every day now breaks
there are people lying dead
tears mix with screams —
Bones clatter and knock
like crabs tightly bound
and roasted for dried meat
those who defend the homefront
children and old soldiers both
brought into this bitterness
And the moving bullet can't be stopped
as it kills all that lives
and insults the dead,
again and again with falling bombs —
thus cremated and burned to ash
Until the grave
that final resting place
is just a cave where they hide . . .
every day now breaks
Somewhere in Vietnam . . .

Because I implore you
and humbly beg you
to gather names

to stop the war
and abolish forever its threat
No teasing, may it never be
No joking, because while
Somewhere in Vietnam
Every day now splits
The stranger rules
and seeks ways to seize control
And so the home country is taken
those who are unable to live as one
destroy each other
like the men who criticize in secret
with thoughts of begging
For Peace, they say,
knowing it is sought
with guns and pride
that destroy the earth
as has been the custom . . .

They say that in order for "truth"
They say that in order for "justice"
we are pounded and beaten
smeared and covered with mud
strangled and sown
by those who love the homeland.
And now the most dangerous —
brothers born of the same mother
pushed until they begin to split . . .

Each day now splits
Somewhere in Vietnam . . .

And now I demand and plead,
I beg this from my soul

Let us be together
Let us gather signatures
To cease and desist
The war going on
In that place Vietnam

—M. Rado
(Ivato/Antananarivo)

৩৩৩৩৩

Afrika!

It is better that bones splinter
Let the blood overflow
Dear Afrika
If this makes the dew
That wets
The constricted throat
To speak in anger
Until it was spent
Until freedom is sought

The wound is nothing
Because strength left in the bosom
Must get out in one violent effort
And rise

For until there is gasping
And something flexible
In the small breath pressing close

And the thin muscles, the only remnant free to move about
Never again durable, only this weakness used by the enemy

And so leap up
And come down, speak precisely
As if searching for lice
Turn aside
And so put in action the deceit of war
To distract the enemy

Use surprise
To strike with the knife
When challenged

Forge ahead and everyone clench your teeth
Freedom is there in the distant brightness

The blackness of your skin
Is not the wrong day
How is it that you
Renowned as the land of the sun
Again are not getting life's fair share

Have trust
Because I am here your brother
To throw the rope, release the knife and stones
Against our enemies for the sake of freedom

And that I dare is my dare
Dear Afrika my brother

—M. Rado
(Ivato/Antananarivo)

People of the Highlands, Long Valleys, and Thorns   149

ৰ৵ ৰ৵ ৰ৵ ৰ৵ ৰ৵

Maliciousness *

I invited death
last night,
but it did not arrive!
Did not appear.
Disdained my thirst
that wanted to caress those frigid hands cold as death
death I wanted to substitute for the hot kiss
my beloved betrayed me with last night!

Malicious!

I summoned life,
but it did not come!
Abandoned I will be soaked
there I was myself in that false life:
Alive already dead,
for the echo of my love is never to be heard.

Malicious!

—M. Rado
(Ivato/Antananarivo)

---

* *Sompatra*—one who is constantly annoying or hurting others, forever committing wanton acts
of destruction.

୭ଚ୭ଚ୭ଚ୭ଚ

Nostalgia *

There but exhausted
My heart lies heavy but why? Daylight already
Trailing evening's dark garments turned aside
With my strength do I grow weary?

Or . . . the bright vision of the past
Filled with coaxing that fades through years?
And is what I predict left dressed to mourn
Far out of sight whatever I wished?

Or . . . on the other hand
Does weariness of mind tear me apart soon
Leaving only strength a wild beast prowling for song
As appeasement?

—M. Rado
(Ivato/Antananarivo)

---

* *Embona*—to remember with sorrow that from which one has been separated,
a child from a parent, a foreigner away from home in Madagascar.

CHAPTER VII

TURNING THE BONES

Nothing reminded me more of being in the Southern Hemisphere than the flip-flop of seasons. By late May, winter was beginning to make its way from the south, and instead of summer breezes, winds carried a tinge of Antarctic air onto a country dotted with palm trees and sweetly scented ylang-ylang. There was no snow, but in the mornings the air was crisp enough to let me see my breath, and in the garden bordering the veranda each flower petal held a dollop of frost like a sequin left by a sprite. By the end of the month, Mme. Arianne had begun ordering a fire to warm us while we had dinner on the veranda. The cobalt blue of the evening sky was sueded with winter light. Sparks from the dry wood danced in the cool air before dying in a sprinkle of ash among bamboo and liana vines. With the drop in temperature, the sight of bright red blooms on poinsettia trees, standing tall as magnolias or willows, made me think of home, Thanksgiving, and those green plastic pots of poinsettias my mother would buy from a florist to grace the dining room table. But in Madagascar, poinsettias grew on trees that reached heights of ten feet or more, and winter had come in May, the sun playing hide-and-seek through a thin veil of high clouds above the hills outside Antananarivo.

We had passed through the rainy season and into winter. The ground was dry, and the only moisture in the air was condensed in fog that would hang near the ground until midday, when the sun reclaimed the land for a few hours. All in all, the climate was perfect for a *famadihana*, a visit to the ancestors.

"The diviner has decided the day is most auspicious," Mme. Arianne told me. "You are lucky to be invited to the ceremony of the ancestors."

Lucky indeed, I thought, as I buttoned my sweater up to my neck, and silently thanked the guardians of weather. I had been out of bed for only two days after a bout with malaria, and I didn't want my body to mistake the nip in the air for the chills and fever that had sent me to bed for a week. So I was well aware that my first bit of luck was to have recovered in time to attend a *famadihana*. The ceremony was being conducted by friends of Mme. Arianne's, and she had managed to secure an invitation for me. My second stroke of luck was that this *famadihana* was being held at the end of May instead of the usual schedule of late winter, which for the Southern Hemisphere occurred in June or July. As the diviner had said: the day was most auspicious.

From the veranda, I watched thin fingers of fog trace the rooftops of houses perched on the hillside beneath us. Fog drifted toward the central part of the capital city, where the upper floors of government buildings were shrouded in mist. It was still morning, not quite six o'clock, and I needed my sweater and the cup of hot sweet tea that Mme. Arianne had prepared for me. I had just finished the last sip when Tiana rang the bell to the outside gate to signal that Simon, our driver, was waiting. I checked my shoulder bag. Medicine to keep the malaria at bay, my camera, recorder and notebook, a scarf to keep out the morning chill, and an umbrella for the afternoon sun. I picked up the lunch Mme. Arianne had prepared and gingerly made my way down the steeply winding steps—103 of them—to the street.

"You are not yet well, so be careful," Mme. Arianne warned. I told her I would, but that precaution had occurred to me immediately after I'd started my descent down the stairs. Not only did I realize I was just beginning to regain my sense of balance, but the specter of shivering and sweating was all too fresh in my memory. Still in less than an hour, I found myself caught up in *famadihana*, the "turning of the bones," and nearly forgot my recent illness.

As Simon maneuvered the Renault along the outer rim of the Zoma market past the rush of cars, busses, and pousse-pousse freight carriers, I could see the row of vendors selling funeral lambas, some woven out of rough burlap, and others from silk or finely stitched cotton.

"I want to buy one," I had told Tiana one day as we strolled through the market.

She had laughed at me. "No, no," she said. "It is not possible. It is *fady*, taboo. This is only for the dead. For the ancestors."

"But one day I will need one," I said. "I must be prepared."

She had laughed again, but when she saw I was serious, told me, "This lamba is only for the family to buy, to honor the ancestors. That is how the living take care of the dead."

And that morning, as we drove past the Zoma, Tiana nodded toward the stalls of funeral lambas. "Today, you will see how we use these *lambamena* for the dead," she told me.

For once, I mentally urged Simon to drive at the usual Malagasy breakneck speed, but on the congested streets near the market, traffic crept at a pace that was almost a standstill. We were stuck behind buses and trucks belching diesel fumes with each bounce along the cobblestones. Occasionally, traffic was delayed even more by runners pulling pousse-pousse carts loaded with cargo. In some places where the streets were too narrow to allow even the smallest cars to pass slower vehicles, the pousse-pousse made better time than the Renault.

We drove to a section of the capital I had never visited, one of Tana's outlying districts laced with cobblestone streets. I was struck first by the change in architectural design. Here, in Tana's suburb, the houses were squat, gray adobe, and drab compared to the brightly colored residences stacked on the hillsides of downtown Tana, or the narrow russet-colored railroad houses of the Highlands. In Tana's suburb, the houses were less imposing than those on the road to Antsirabe, and most of them were roofed with tin rather than in the red tiles that crowned the villas and pensions in the heart of town.

Indeed, this part of the city was more village than urban. Instead of the verandas and French garden walls common to the area around the Zoma Market, the houses were box-like structures, with small, shuttered windows, and doorways that opened directly onto the street. Occasionally, I heard a chicken cackling in the fenced-in space between houses, or caught a glimpse of a scrawny dog crouched under a tree. I was ready to convince myself that the city was somewhere far behind when Simon turned into a driveway that opened onto a courtyard. We had entered the gates of a Carmelite convent, and suddenly, in contrast to the street we'd just left, we were surrounded by buildings that bore inescapable traces of Europe.

At first glance, the courtyard seemed no more remarkable than any convent or monastery I'd seen in other parts of the world. I had that same sense of being enclosed that I always had, a feeling that people were being kept out rather than invited in. The buildings were square and officious, their windows more utilitarian than placed to capture the view of the surrounding countryside. The courtyard was framed by a church, a school, a dormitory, the main office, and an infirmary. A statue of the Virgin Mary stood vigil over one end of the driveway, and the convent's church, adorned with a ten foot cross, was visible behind a hillock directly in front of the building facing the gate. But this was no ordinary convent. What made it unique was the tomb that was nested on the slope of the hillock, a tomb that was unmistakably Malagasy, although less impressive than the concrete block mausoleums I'd seen on the hillsides above the highway south of town. The hillside tombs that dotted the landscape throughout the Highlands were small rectangular structures made visible for miles by a fresh coat of whitewash to honor the ancestors who govern the living from their vantage point in eternity. The tomb in the convent's courtyard was modest by comparison, so unpretentious I might not have noticed it on any other day, probably because most of it, like a prairie root cellar, was below ground. Just an extra projection, more like a scattering of stones on a scraggly rise of ground shaded by aging *amontana*, sycamore trees, but inside, the *razana*, the ancestors, were cradled in the heart of the earth. In contrast to the severity of the convent's buildings, the tomb assumed the same contours of the earth around it, lending even more reverence to its presence.

"The nuns have told the family that they need to use the land," Tiana said. "They need it to expand the buildings of the convent, but only the family can legally remove the bodies. So the nuns have made an urgent petition and that is why the family is holding the ceremony early. Today they will move their ancestors to a new tomb on sacred ground in the hills."

The nuns peered at us through the windows of the convent's dormitory, but stayed within the confines of their walls. Groups of men were already clearing dirt from the entryway and from a path around the tomb in preparation for the family to enter the vault. Women arranged the bundles of *lambamena* and outer shrouds, and kept an eye on the children who were impatient for events to begin. But no one approached the nuns. We all waited for the immediate family who would bring the diviner and family elder to signal the beginning of the *famadihana*.

I took a seat on a bench near the driveway under the spreading limbs of a ylang-ylang tree. The blossoms were heavy with fragrance, and the scent of plumeria brought back memories of Hawaii. Perhaps it was the scent of flowers that made the unfamiliar seem familiar; but whatever the reason, I began to feel that I was indeed a part of what was going on around me.

More than once while I was in Madagascar, I found myself measuring the thin line between family and stranger, especially when I was mistaken for Malagasy, my facial features reminding someone of a Betsileo or Bara friend, or a Sakalava neighbor. Of course, I only needed to attempt a few words in Malagasy, laminated by my midwestern accent, for anyone to recognize that I was a *vahiny*, a stranger. But nevertheless, I was asked, sometimes simply because I resembled a friend who had recently immigrated to the West, or the child or perhaps the grandchild of that person. And always, even when I was asked how far had I traveled and how long would I stay, I was an outsider made to feel welcome.

That was how I felt the morning of the *famadihana*—a stranger in a world that was at once both familiar and foreign, a *vahiny* who was as moved by this gathering as I would have been by a wake held by my own family. I remembered my grandfather's wake, the relatives who had journeyed to St. Louis from all over the United States, the mixture of joy and sadness as we shared a meal of my grandfather's favorite food and listened to stories of his life, both truth and fiction. It was our way of acknowledging that my grandfather had passed on and would no longer be a part of our lives except in memory. Such was not the case with the *famadihana*. This was no funeral, no *funèrailles des morts*. There were no somber clothes, no women veiled in black or men in stiff suits. Children played *fangalam-piery*, and grown-ups made preparations to properly greet the ancestors. There was an air of expectancy, an urgency to get on with the business of the day, business that this day included "turning the bones."

By the time the rest of the family arrived, only the shadows bore traces of the morning dew, but in the widening patches of sunlight, heat chased away the chill. During the twenty-five minutes while I was sitting on the bench in the courtyard of the Carmelite convent, I had prepared myself to wait, thinking that like most family gatherings, at least the ones held by my family, the bulk of the morning would be taken up with negotiating which task would be assigned to whom. By my estimation, this might take some time, since by then the group totaled about forty or so adults and at least half as many children, and I imagined that all of them would have an opinion about the order of things.

When the diviner and family elder emerged from the last caravan of cars to enter the courtyard, everyone, except the nuns, converged upon the hillock as if by a prearranged signal. All idle conversation ceased. Even the children who had been playing catch-me games in the driveway

Diviner and elder at Famadihana, near Antananarivo

moved closer to their parents, who were standing near the tomb. Then, the Mother Superior came out to speak to the family elder, M. Razanatsimba. After a brief discussion, she returned to the convent office, and M. Razanatsimba joined the diviner, M. Rakotoarisoa, in front of the doorway to the tomb.

The family elder, M. Razanatsimba, with his salt and pepper hair and neatly trimmed mustache, reminded me of one of my father's army buddies who had served with him in World War II. In the summers, after my father retired from the military, they would come to our house and help him fill the backyard with stories of their army days. The young boys in the neighborhood, who would sometimes stop by for a visit, listened avidly. I watched M. Razanatsimba go about his duties, directing the younger men through the final stages of opening the tomb. He moved with the ease of authority that no one questioned. When the door was released, he beckoned to the diviner, M. Rakotoarisoa. They seemed a most appropriate team, the diviner and the elder. M. Rakotoarisoa, who was about the same height as the elder, was clean shaven and wore a jaunty fedora, and like the elder, was dressed casually in a sport coat and a shirt, open at the throat. Both men could have been on their way to a friend's house or to a meeting to discuss the political issues of the day, but here they were charged with the governance of a ritual. As the tomb was opened, M. Rakotoarisoa began to speak.

"He is addressing the ancestors," Tiana said. "He tells them that we are their descendants and not as wise as they are. He is apologizing for disturbing them, but he asks them to be patient with us. He tells them that they will be taken to a new place. He says the ancestors are wise and if we are careful, they have much to tell us."

I watched the family milling around the tomb. Once M. Rakotoarisoa had finished speaking, everyone seemed to have something to say, not loudly but with a murmuring of conversation. Everyone wanted to look into the newly opened tomb, to add their voice to the comments already filling the air. As I watched the men about to enter the tomb, I realized a few people were looking my way, not staring but rather checking my reaction. I smiled. They smiled back. I was measuring that line between friend and stranger again, but at the unspoken invitation of several people, I moved forward and looked into the tomb.

The air that greeted me was cool and dry and smelled of earth, like moss or leaves turning to mulch. The room was dark, unlit even by the rays of sunlight breaking through the last traces of fog. But I felt no sense of uneasiness, no dread of spirits about to rise and take hold of me. Instead, I sensed a kind of peacefulness, as if I had been invited into the parlor of a house reserved only for very special guests. I leaned forward for a closer look. The walls seemed carved out of the very earth itself, with niches along the sides and a corridor down the middle for easy passage, the space seemingly measured with an exacting fit for several generations of the family. There were no labels, no conventional tombstones, only the dim outlines of bodies wrapped in *lambamena* and outer shrouds woven of sisal. I stepped back from the opening and watched as the men began the procession of ancestors. They started with the eldest.

"How can they know who is lying where?" I asked.

"I must know where each ancestor rests," M. Razanatsimba told me. His English was halting but clear. And when he was unsure of a word, Tiana translated for him. "*Famadihana* is the responsibility of the eldest," he continued. "This is *fombandrazana*, the ways of the ancestors."

When M. Rakotoarisoa, who could speak only Malagasy, added a comment, Tiana told me, "He is saying that there is order in everything and it is *fady* to disturb that order. The eldest must observe what is *fady*, what is taboo."

"You see, everyone has a role," M. Razanatsimba said. "The men will lift each one from the tomb. They must all be greeted and offered new lambas, silk ones to honor them. Each one, each one will have a new lamba and a place in the new tomb."

"The diviner says that today is the best day," Tiana told me. "The weather is cool and the space between sky and earth is clear. No rain. The best weather for *famadihana*."

M. Rakotoarisoa smiled at the prospect of such an auspicious day for the ceremony. "Yes, it is a good day," M. Razanatsimba added. "Everyone is ready."

I watched the men enter the tomb, and a few seconds later, reemerge with the remains of an ancestor. Even after years in earthen beds, the shrouds looked surprisingly intact. The procession moved swiftly, the men placing the oldest ancestor in the laps of three or four of the youngest descendants seated on the ground, their legs stretched out in front of them. As soon as one body was positioned in the laps of the family, the men returned to the tomb for the next one. This process was broken only once when they excavated the remains of an infant who had been buried outside of the tomb because it had not lived long enough to be considered an ancestor. (In order to make the journey to the new tomb, the child was nestled in the arms of its deceased father, who would now be its guardian in the world of the ancestors.) Soon there was a lineup, twelve ancestors in all, and the family seated on the ground, cradling them like students at their desks, or worshipers in church pews.

As each body was put in place, the old folks chastised the young. "Be careful," they called. "Hold the cloth straight. Who has grandfather? Who has mother?"

The youngsters who were seated along the last row, and given the duty to hold the oldest of the ancestors, lifted the edges of the shrouds. "It is their grandfather or great-grandfather," Tiana said. I watched them examine the remains. There were no bones, no gruesome skeletons set in ghastly repose. What was uncovered looked more like tree bark, the color of earth or fresh loam in a newly plowed field. "They wonder which end is the head and which the feet," Tiana said. I moved closer, my camera focusing on the group. Young girls giggled into the lens while older women offered me a hint of a smile. I obliged them with a photograph. The mood I captured was one of anticipation, the honor to be part of an ancestral ritual. I took a series of photos of the men transferring ancestors from the old shrouds to the new ones. From the more delicate inner shroud of silk or finely woven cotton, the men would tear a strip of material for binding to secure the newly shrouded remains before placing it on the rougher middle *lambamena*, which in turn would be encased in the outer wrapping of sisal. The men worked their way down the rows until they reached the youngest family members, who were still undecided as to which end was officially the feet and which the head. Finally, they made a decision, apologizing to the ancestors for having the foreshortened vision of those who are still living.

One by one, the newly shrouded bodies were made ready for the journey to the new tomb. When everything was in order, the two dozen or so vehicles formed a cortege that would wend its way out of the suburbs of Tana and into the hills where other tombs held reign over the land of the living. As Simon drove us away from the convent grounds, I turned to the back window and caught a glimpse of the nuns running toward the excavation site, all of them leaning forward as if to see if we had forgotten anyone.

It was winter in the Highlands. In the hills above Tana, the grass was as dry and yellow as Kansas wheatfields during a drought. The noonday sun was high in the sky and out there in the open of plateau country, we could feel the sun's heat. The bodies were placed on sawhorses under the sparse shade of a few *ampaly* trees. While we had lunch, the family paid their respects to various ancestors, telling them of recent events, of regrets and unions, of desires and rapprochements. By early afternoon, when the family lined up to shoulder the weight of their ancestors, jackets were removed and shirt sleeves were rolled up. They were preparing for the processional that would usher the ancestors into the new tomb. The musicians pulled out their instruments and the women began their songs of loss and family and trust. The diviner officiated in the sacrifice of a rooster, and the elder released the door of the new tomb with a cast-iron key the size of a pair of pliers. The family carried newly shrouded bodies on their shoulders like pallbearers at a wake. Seven times they circled the tomb. The bandleader directed the musicians, who played the music of storytellers and dancers. The mood was both serious and upbeat. Some complained about the weight of an ancestor, the duty of carrying their burden, feet first, seven times in a circle that seemed to widen and shrink erratically. "We must confuse them so that they don't get up and wander away from the tomb," Tiana said. The trumpet player all but drowned out her words. The drummer kept everyone moving. When they saw my camera, they smiled and laughed, beckoned me to join them. "I should have taken a lighter load," someone called. Someone else waved at me. And a *ramatoa*, an older woman, begged the forgiveness of the ancestors for such laughing disrespect. But for that time, while the ancestors took one more outing in the sun, while the diviner entrusted everyone with the responsibility of family and God, while the elder made sure the bodies would be properly placed within the tomb, everyone, with all the music and laughter and singing, everyone was in accord.

Famadihana musician leading parade of ancestors around the tomb, near Antananarivo

For the Malagasy, death is not an end but a beginning of a new role—a role, as M. Razanatsimba had said, "where those who have gone before, continue to be consulted for their wisdom and regard." This tradition generates every stage of life, each marked by sacred rituals: birth, circumcision or initiation, marriage, funerals, and *famadihana*, the "turning of the bones." Each is a lengthy ritual. The traditional marriage proposal, for example, can begin with a five-page metaphorically built plea of intent, written by the groom but presented to the bride's family by his father or grandfather. This proposal constitutes the official agreement of marriage, although the bride has privately accepted the groom's proposal and the groom has secured his position by extending gifts (his "dowry") to the family, and especially to the bride's brothers, where the gifts must be of enough value to "blind them" to the groom's intention of taking their sister from the family. Proposal, gifts, and dowry must be presented with sincerity, solemnity, and respect for the ancestors, although it is the living—the bride's family—who ultimately accept or reject the proposal. Regardless of what other religious or civil ceremonies are performed, it is this traditional ritual that marks the official marriage agreement. For it is there, as each family offers an apology to the ancestors against the presumptions of those who are living, that the bride takes her place among her husband's familial ranks of ancestry.

At no time are the ancestors excluded from Malagasy life. At an elegant dinner party at the home of a professor at the University of Madagascar in Tana, the host, a business executive, included the ancestors in the first toast of the evening by offering the first few drops of wine in the northeastern corner of the house. "For the ancestors," he said. And while no one made further mention of ancestors, I felt their presence, not unpleasantly but understandably, throughout the evening. It was one of the times during my visit when, once more, I found myself considering how far I was from home. In the United States the dead are locked in memory and beseeched to "rest in peace." They have "passed over," "passed away." They are out of our lives. Only as an adult had I brought my grandfather back into the realm of the living through my writing. And only when I began to write about him did I realize how much I'd felt his absence during my childhood. But the Malagasy live with, and at death join, their ancestors. To die away from home, away from the land of the ancestors, is an unthinkable proposition.

This was made clear to me the afternoon we landed in Toliara. The flight already had been delayed one day because of an airline workers' strike, so the additional time it took us to reach Toliara was not surprising until we landed and the passengers began walking toward the terminal. It was then that I noticed a large group of people walking out of the terminal and heading for the plane. Women in bright lambas, who could be going to the market, except they were weeping. Young women of extraordinary beauty, walking close to their mothers and grandmothers, and all of them, young and old, sobbing loudly. Young men with stern, sad faces, some of them supporting older men who seemed on the verge of collapsing. Tears flowed from the eyes of even a small child who was clinging to his mother's side.

"Someone is coming home," Tiana said.

I turned. The plane stood with its cargo door open, and as the people surged onto the runway, an airline regulation coffin was lowered onto a cart. Then I remembered the curtain covering two rows of seats in the forward cabin. And I remembered how at Antananarivo I'd noticed the ground crew loading the plane from the cargo hatch of an international flight.

"Someone has died in Europe or America," Tiana said. "Sometimes the family must wait for years to have the money to bring them home. But it doesn't matter where you die," Tiana told me, "because for the Malagasy, you must come home and take your place among the ancestors. Only then can your family mourn you."

"Yes. Someone has come home," I said, and walked toward the exit where our day was about to begin.

*Raha very kely, manontany razana; fa raha very
lehibe, manontany fanompoana.*
When what's left is small, we ask the
ancestors, but when what's left is large,
we pray.

ဆာဆာဆာဆာဆာ

*Andriananahary (Zanahary) sy Andriantompo:
The Lord Who Creates and the Lord Who Owns*

A long time ago, at the beginning, what the Malagasy people call
Andriananahary or Zanahary, the Lord Who Creates, reigned in the
Heavens and Andriantompo, the Lord Who Owns, reigned on the earth.
One day, Andriantompo, the Lord Who Owns, decided to knead clay
mud into a shape that shows our own features but could not move. At
that time, Andriantompo was still on good terms with Andriananahary.
So Andriantompo consulted with Andriananahary, or as he is some-
times called, Zanahary.

"What can we do with this shaped mud?" he asked.

Andriananahary replied, "We can give it breath."

And Andriananahary did so, and the kneaded clay could breathe
and move. Since then, what we call *olombelona*, or human beings, were
created.

The days, months, and years elapsed and the good friendship between
Andriananahary and Andriantompo turned into a wave of misunderstanding and anger. So Andriananahary, or Zanahary, who gave the
breath and the life said, "I'm going to take the *olombelona* away, because
it was I who had given them breath and life." Andriantompo answered
back, "You have no right to take the *olombelona* away, because it was I
who had given them a body and shape." Since that fight between Andri-

ananahary and Andriantompo, what we call Rafahafatesana or Death appeared (which in Malagasy is personified by the use of the prefix *Ra-*). Andriananahary took the breath and life away, and Andriantompo kept and destroyed the body which is what happens when we face Death.

In some respects, when the Malagasy people die, the euphemistic term "Taken away by He (Andriananahary/Zanahary) who had given the life" will be used to say that the person is dead; while the body that is believed to stay, since it belongs to Andriantompo, will be respectfully called Ratompokovavy [*Ra-*: marks the respect to somebody; *Tompoko*: my owner/my lord; *Vavy*: woman/girl] or Ratompokolahy [for *Lahy*: man/boy], which indirectly implies that the body belongs to my owner [woman/man]. These terms are used to entitle the deceased persons.

The Malagasy people respect deceased persons, since the life is given back to Andriananahary and the body is given back to Andriantompo. The breath and the body go to the place where each supposedly holds a very important and authoritative position. This belief preserves and reinforces what the Malagasy people call *fifankatiavana*, or friendship/relationship. The Malagasy people believe that the life given back to Andriananahary (Zanahary), as well as the holy body given back to Andriantompo, produces the power to communicate with them. For that specific reason, the Malagasy people are extremely respectful of their late relatives.

This belief, however, suggests the importance of a good relationship among relatives during a lifetime, to deny the veracity of the saying *Maty vao ramalala* (referring to an ostentatious love or consideration paid to a person after his/her death when there was no respect during life). This good relationship is often praised by saying: "Is elder brother/sister redolent of flowers?" or "Is younger brother/sister redolent of leaves, that makes the house redolent of the Prince (Death)?" The reply should be: "No, it is not elder brother/sister who is redolent of flowers; it is not younger brother/sister who is redolent of fragrant leaves, but so strong is

the kinship/friendship that it makes the house redolent of the Prince."
For that reason, the Malagasy people never abandon their relatives,
and that notion of wisdom is often transmitted to the younger generation through storytelling, which is, most of the time, based on giving
each other some sort of education for social harmony. This philosophy
also explains the reason why the Malagasy people perform the ritual of
famadihana; that is, they remove (and take care of) the corpse from one
tomb to another, because the Malagasy people do not want to lose those
who are gone, since the deceased also take good care of those who remain.

However, the Malagasy people seem ambiguous regarding funerals
and family tombs, even though the current proverb says, *Velona iray
trano; maty iray fasana* (Alive, we live in the same house; dead, we lie
down in the same grave). The fact of sharing the same tomb is sometimes
questionable, since people in the same family may not be buried in the
same family tomb. The family tomb serves as the diary of the Malagasy
people. It is the place of the ancestors and holds their stories.

—Ernest Rakotosamala
(Fianarantsoa)

CHAPTER VIII

THE LIGHT STILL
SHINES TOMORROW

On the western shores of Madagascar, near the town of Mahajanga, the tide carries fingers of red soil out to the Chanel de Mozambique. This rosy laterite, washed down from the sea cliffs, unfurls on the surf like blood— a banner of red edging onto the lip of the world. As we walked down the trail to the beach, I could only think of a Picasso painting: the sky unbelievably blue, the cliffs like layer cakes of clay and sand stretching the length of the windblown coast, the sun baking those fingers of drifting red soil into an even brighter fluorescence. We had slipped past the decaying fences of villas that had been vacated by the French, past the high-tide scrabble of broken shells and crabgrass, past the anchor of beached fishing pirogues and down to the plateau of sand at Amborovy Beach, where water and soil finally mingled in ever-darkening lines of fuchsia and crimson. The sun was relentless, baking all colors into some shade of red on the hot sand, and the heat was accentuated by a chergui wind that blew puffs of red dust, like exclamation marks. I had opened my umbrella, but even under its shade, the heat seeped through my clothes with every gust of wind.

Perhaps it was the open umbrella, and the sand and sea around me, that made me think of Picasso—that photo of the painter's wife walking behind him on the beach under the shade of a parasol. But it was not the umbrella alone. There were also the colors, a palette of hues in ocher, red, and pink, the endless blue sky crowning sudden white flecks of foam along the waves at the horizon. What painter would not have envied the brilliance of colors bound in timeless unity in a place of such incredible beauty?

We walked from the bramble of sand and reed grass at the edge of the villas to the blood-dyed waters along the shore. Colors shimmered and danced in the heat. We were alone on the beach, the heat skinning our legs until we reached the water's edge. This was a place where chameleons and birds of prey relived their dreams of the sea, while the wind-scoured Highlands drained red soil onto the savannah, a swath that spread itself from the foothills to the rivers, leaving desert and forest huddled just out of reach of the ocean. This was the land of bejeweled crocodiles, gentle ghosts, and patient fishermen.

My visit to Mahajanga was fraught with both good luck and a host of complications. My luck began immediately, because not only was Mahajanga Tiana's hometown, but the first cab driver we hired, Arthur Ravelomanatsoa, was a recent graduate of the University. "To open a practice in dentistry, this takes money," he said. "So now, I drive a taxi." He took us on a tour of Mahajanga, along the wide Avenue de France that followed the curve of the seashore. The boulevard was bordered with coconut palms and banked with a seawall—the water glimmering on one side of the road and the line of palms beckoning on the other side. At one point along the esplanade, the road had been cut to circumvent a massive baobab tree, said to be seven hundred years old. It majestically rose two or three stories high and was over forty feet at the base. Above its short, wide trunk, branches spread out like a giant awning, a canopy of louvered light falling through the thick leaves.

Arthur said. "If you need to meet someone, just tell them, 'Under the baobab' and they will be waiting here."

"Many lovers come to this place," Tiana added. And I thought of how it must be under a violet-colored evening sky with the air laundered by breezes from the sea. Perfect for lovers.

We walked around the tree, taking pictures of this angle and that but never able to hold the entire span of the baobab in the camera's lens no matter what angle we tried. The waves lapping against the seawall a few feet away seemed to laugh at our efforts. We left the baobab and followed the road south until we came to the harbor at Pointe de Sable, where dock workers loaded and unloaded cargoes of rice, cashews, spices, and cattle, and fishermen weighed their catch of the day. Crates of cargo, and loose coconuts piled like small pyramids, waited to be loaded. Light slipped through the lace of cargo nets in checkerboard patterns. Along one wharf, sailors readied the dhows for their next oceangoing voyage. The men, harnessed in cowhide cradles, leaned in crazy angles from the sun as they scraped the sides of the ships. It was a busy port: the comings and go-ings of cattle and produce, men and boats clocked to take advantage of the tides.

That evening we drove to the northern end of Avenue de France, and in the Village Touristique on the jetty at Pointe du Caiman, we had din-ner. The water was streaked in various shades of red, and fishing pi-rogues, coming into port, seemed to be floating on a crayon sea. A hunting party returned to the hotel restaurant just as the horizon began to swal-low the last rays of light. The party was a mixed bunch of white South Africans and Australians, loudly full of themselves because they had bagged a wild boar and several pheasant-like birds. While their Mala-gasy guides stabled the horses and brought in the game and equipment, the hunters, looking more like an old-time safari group than tourists flown in for only a week, ordered endless rounds of beer. It was whispered that they'd also captured some turtles, but they weren't drunk enough to display any endangered species. After we left the smoke-filled restaurant, the night air, with its lingering smells of flowers and salt water, seemed even sweeter.

The next day, we drove through cashew and rice fields to Lake Mangatsa, the sacred lake. Without Arthur to guide us, we would not have found the route to Mangatsa. Maps never clearly designated its location, and the road all but disappeared into a gravel path of overgrown marsh reeds. From a distance, it was difficult to see that there was even a clearing, much less a small lake full of lily pads and sizable fish. But the trees bordering the lake were festooned with ribbons of white and red cloth. As we drew closer, I saw several bottles and jars placed at the base of some of the trees as offerings or prayers. Arthur began to tear pieces of bread from the fresh baguette he'd bought in the market before we'd left Mahajanga.

"No one fishes this lake," he said. "It is *fady* because our ancestors are here."

I looked into the water. Swimming among the lily pads were some of the largest fish I'd ever seen outside of the goldfish in Buddhist pools in Japan, where it was also forbidden to disturb the fish. Like the goldfish in the temples in Japan, the fish in Lake Mangatsa were more than symbols of spirituality. According to beliefs, they are reincarnations of the ancestors and protectors of their descendants.

"Many politicians come here to seek the advice of the ancestors," Tiana said.

"Yes," Arthur added, "and one who tried to build an embankment on the lake broke the *fady* and was punished because he did not respect the ancestors. The ribbons you see, and the jars of rum and honey, they are all offerings to the ancestors." We walked to one of the trees where several cloths had writings on them. "Like prayers," he said. "The trees are also sacred."

Streaks of tangerine-orange and palomino-colored fish came quickly to the surface for Arthur's offering of baguette. They'd feed, drift under the lilies, come back for another crust of bread, drift away again. They moved as if they knew they were protected. "I hope they will think kindly of us," I said.

After we left the lake, we visited a nearby village, more a group of houses than a village. Everyone was in the rice fields when we arrived, but Arthur went out to beckon them. The men stayed in the fields but eight or so women came to greet us. Arthur gave them photographs from the last research group that had passed through, and they posed for pictures with us. When we left, they waved goodby and asked us to come back after the planting season. "Only if Arthur will bring us," I said. We drove back to Mahajanga through fields of saffron flowers and cinammon, our car no more than a metallic flicker in the yellow-green light.

Living up to its Swahili name, *mji angaïa*, city of flowers, Mahajanga was resplendent with bougainvillea, orchids, Flaming Katy, and jasmine. Flittering among the blossoms were honeybees, butterflies, and lizards, those patient guardians of time. When we visited the Catholic school Tiana had attended as a child, I watched one watching us. We stood across the street from the school as students left for their noonday meal. The bright green Parson's chameleon clung to a branch, its ridged back sloping down to the tail wrapped around the limb like a tendril of hair. I hadn't seen it at first, had been too distracted by the flowers—bright periwinkles and yellow blooms like buttercups. Then two schoolgirls had paused to have their pictures taken, the wind ruffling their flowered cotton dresses. As they giggled into the lens, the chameleon had blinked, a brief second that broke his studied silence but enough to give me time to focus. Then it took one slow step—steathily as if sizing up my presence—and with a churlish toss of its head, vanished. I had been lucky. My camera was already set, so I'd grabbed a shot before it took flight.

I was not always as lucky with gathering stories, or at least, the stories I sought were not always the ones I uncovered. Such was the case later that afternoon when we made the first of two visits to a Boina settlement, part of the Sakalava kingdom in the western section of Madagascar. From the road, the fencing around the settlement looked no different than that surrounding other houses in the area. Perhaps the hedge of flowering thornbushes was a bit longer and the stand of bamboo a bit thicker, but under the profusion of flowers, the barrier was similar to that of other garden walls. Once we pushed inside the bent-twig gate, the world was quite different.

Mahajanga may have had the air of a seaport, with its bustling of ocean-bound cargo vessels and tourist trade, but inside the Boina settlement, the business of the day followed more traditional lines. The settlement was a rectangular area of small houses with a wide lawn space in front. Like the rest of Mahajanga, there were flowers everywhere, and several fruit trees, in full bloom, graced the neatly groomed yard, that was not so much a lawn as a way of separating the houses from the immediacy of the road. Respectfully, we waited to be asked into the guest house. Two women came to the door to look us over. I was accustomed to seeing lambas wrapped in a Malayo-Polynesian style, like a pareau, but these women wrapped their lambas in the style of North African women, around the waist, leaving enough cloth so that one end could be pulled up to cover the head. In the sun's heat, I began to wish for my own cowl. I fanned at a few insistent flies. One woman patted her hair and smiled at me. Her hair was braided like mine, but rather than leaving it in loose braids, she wore her long braids gathered into two buns, one coiled above each ear. I noticed one of the women had her face decorated with Mangary pigment, a whitish powder that had been drawn in a beautifully intricate pattern of concentric circles, like flowers, with scrollwork lines completing the design.

"This decoration on the face is for medicine and beauty," Tiana said. "Women who do this follow tradition."

The women watched us but kept their distance, and as soon as a man—a mediator, Tiana told me—came to the door, they went around the house to the path where the other dwellings were. Instead of inviting us inside, the man gestured to a shady area under one of the trees. I looked for insects before sitting down, but found none—at least none of the notoriously large varieties I had encountered when we visited Toliara and Fort Dauphin. Once seated, we accepted the mediator's offer of tea to sweeten our conversation.

Although (or perhaps, because) our contact had been arranged through the Ministry of Culture, our timing was off. We had arrived in June, in the middle of preparations for the month-long ceremony to honor the Boina ancestors. Almost everyone was away, we were told, preparing for the next day's ceremonies. When Tiana explained why we had been granted an audience with a mediator—one of the men who would "do the work" of listening to the ancestors—I responded in English instead of French. As I spoke, the mediator looked directly at me for a second. It would be the only time we'd make eye contact. He was a handsome man, taller than most of the Malagasy men I'd seen in the Highlands or in the South. His facial features reflected Africa more than Southeast Asia. While we talked, children gathered to inspect me. An older woman, their mother, shooed them away.

"Tell him that I want to hear stories," I said. Tiana translated into the dialect of the region. The mediator shook his head. "It is impossible," Tiana said. "Now it is *fady* to speak of the stories."

So we talked instead about the weather, the ocean, and how the water was streaked with red clay. "C'est tres belle," I said. The mediator smiled.

"When will this *fady* end?" I asked. Tiana translated. The mediator shrugged. Tiana said, "Today, it is impossible. Perhaps tomorrow." Several women came into the yard. "I would like to hear the stories of women," I said. Tiana did not translate. "It is impossible," she told me. "This is the time that they talk to the ancestors." The mediator began a long speech. His voice was low, evenly pitched.

"He wants to know where you are from," Tiana said. "He wants to know why you would want stories from him."

I tried to explain, Tiana translated, but the mediator continued to look skeptical. And so it went, this quiet conversation one afternoon in Mahajanga in the shade of a willowy tree for which I had no name of English equivalence. The children came back into the yard, some of them hiding behind their mother's skirts. The women stared openly but made no attempt to join the conversation.

"Tell him I wish to hear the stories that are told every day. The ordinary ones." Tiana translated. The mediator shook his head.

"It is impossible," Tiana said. "He wants to know how long you will be in Mahajanga. Perhaps tomorrow there will be time."

I smiled. "Tomorrow will be fine," I said. The mediator shook his head. "Tomorrow is *fady*," Tiana said. I shrugged. The mediator spoke again. Another long speech. I strained to listen. "It will be expensive," Tiana said. I waited. "He wants two bottles of wine, two packs of cigarettes, two bottles of beer, two bottles of rum, and three thousand francs for the dancers." She paused. "It will be for the ceremony, I think."

I wasn't concerned with what he'd do with the gifts; I was just relieved that he hadn't asked for zebu. I smiled. The *fady* had been lifted, or so I thought. We left with the mediator's promise that he'd talk to us when we returned the next day.

But one day does not necessarily forecast the next. When we returned to the Boina settlement, we were greeted by a different man, an elder. There was no explanation about where the mediator from the previous day might be, but we were expected and immediately invited into the house. This time, the women, five of them, came into the room along with us. They seated themselves along one wall and offered us cushions on the floor in front of them. In spite of the rather formal atmosphere, it was a comfortable room, with a thatched ceiling and walls paneled in strips of wood bound by laths that held the inner walls to the outer walls. It was a sparsely furnished room, containing several tables, and many cushions were covered in Malagasy prints depicting zebu horns, flowers, and birds in crosshatch patterns—almost geometric, definitely bearing a similarity to Arab-African textile designs. A bicycle stood in one corner, and in another corner, material that someone was sewing into a garment. It was a bright room, cooled by a transom breeze caught in the open windows.

The women arranged themselves on cushions near the elder's stool. He was as handsome as the man we'd met the day before: graying at the temples, a neatly trimmed mustache, and intensely bright eyes. He made

Elder, Boina settlement, Mahajanga

eye contact with me immediately, confident in his manner, the kind of man who was accustomed to giving orders. He reminded me of the men in the Masonic Lodge that my father belonged to in St. Louis. He gestured toward the parcels we'd brought, and we deposited our payment. They all inspected the beverages, and one woman, who Tiana said was his wife, began to distribute the cigarettes. The woman smiled "thank you," revealing a gold tooth that signified her importance among the other wives. She caught me glancing at a woman wearing Mangary pigment designs, and gestured to her face, then mine. I shook my head, but told Tiana to ask her to show me how the designs were done. The woman gathered some jars of powder and a mortar bowl from another corner of the room, and, with a cigarette hanging from her mouth like a gambler, began blending the powder into a paste. The elder seemed amused by all of this, but the women smiled. I smiled. Everyone seemed pleased, or so I thought.

"He says he is not in the position to give you stories," Tiana said. "Today is *fady* for such stories."

"Ask him how long the *fady* will last," I said.

"It is very difficult to tell these stories now," Tiana translated. "It is the time for what they call 'bathing the king' that begins in April and ends in September."

"But it's only June!" I said. "And yesterday, we were told to come back today, not September!"

The elder gave me a look that said he clearly did not understand why I was getting so excited. Even the women stopped decorating their faces long enough to stare at me, but as soon as the elder began talking again, they went back to their artwork.

"He will not tell the stories of the people," Tiana translated, "but he will explain the ritual of bathing the king, *Mandoky fandrama*, that everyone is now observing. It is the ritual that makes today *fady* for telling any of the stories."

The elder arranged himself comfortably and began, his style more in the manner of an orator at *hiragasy* than that of the storyteller. But while his oration was not strictly an *angano*, a story, his pacing was like a storyteller's, with dramatic pauses to emphasize the importance of one part of the traditional ceremony over another. There were many pauses, not just to allow time for Tiana's translation, but also to see if I understood the importance of what was being said. And while he recalled the ceremony of *Mandoky fandrama*, the women continued painting their faces with Mangary and did not speak. I listened attentively. I would get this explanation and no more, his eyes told me.

And so we left the settlement with the description of a ceremony that could be traced back to the Boina kingdom of the late seventeenth century. It wasn't the "everyday tale" that I had sought, but it was a story as epic in its nature as the *Iliad*. It was, for the Sakalava, a way of honoring the *razana*—royal ancestors who, it seemed, took scarce notice of women.

ᔆᔆᔆᔆᔆ

The Rite of Bathing the King

The silky earth or the clay of earth is the basis for his food, which is a symbol of his purity. He does not arrive when there is not this pure food. Here in our place every year we celebrate. The rite of bathing the king is the reason that we perform this ceremony each year, not like in Menabe where it is every five years. From the month of January, we follow the calendar to the month of July.

In April we perform *Mitsipa*: cleansing to prevent bad omens, where we must wait to see the full moon. After April, we perform *Fanompoa fandrama*: preparation for what we call "bathing in honey the great-grandfather" (the king's spirit, who we call *Ndremisara*).

When the moon begins to fold in June, this is the time for *Mandoky tao-maity* (what we call "cook the black season") or *Mandoky fandrama* ("to cook the honey"). Then we rest for a month and leave all of this work behind until July, when we have *Mampando*, the ritual of bathing for the great-grandfather, *Ndremisara*, not the ritual for the tomb but here in his house, the palace. When the time comes for bathing on Friday in July, there is a feast.

Afterwards, the guests go home on Saturday and come back a second time in September, when there is no longer a bathing ritual but we resume the ritual of speaking with the spirits which we have left unfinished since July. After September, there are no more rituals again until the next year.

How is this ritual of bathing the king performed? Thursday morning is a taboo. The king's palace is not open, although there is another place to receive those who would visit. Friday is the day of the ritual. On Saturday, we must prepare for the actual bathing of the king. On Sunday, the people from the country come together. On Monday, we send for the mediator, someone who travels to the South, who is a kind of servant for the spirits and who handles the conversation. This is the one who reports everything to the spirits. Then after that they may commune with the king and his royal descendants and those with power or authority.

We appoint this person to carry his share, to commune with them for three hours and, afterwards, report back to the people. Then the ritual is complete, and we feast, happily dancing and doing everything we ought to do to celebrate.

Fitampoha, the ritual of bathing the king, is difficult to speak about. Even though you say *fitampoha*, the action of bathing the king, the highest royalty and the king's ancestors, but really, every day the king is symbolically taking his bath. When he eats a meal, we don't say "eats a meal" but *mihaja*, "he honors himself." Or when he sleeps in the daytime or at night, we say *mirotsy izy*, "he soothes himself." And when he dies, we don't say dead but *Folaka Mpanjaka*: "The king is broken but still holding together. He has turned his back on us." The status of the royalty is a different [kind of] ancestral descent. When the king is broken, we wait a month or two before the burial, but it is called *mitangirika*, "to be secreted." Women cannot enter the crypt of the king.

—as told in Mahajanga (Boina settlement)

Although my visit to the Boina settlement was mired in traditional taboos, luck was with me when I visited Aranta, a tiny fishing village on Bombetoka Bay, the apron of Mahajanga's coast. Arthur deposited us on a weed-covered lot at the foot of a narrow lane between two small houses, built so close to each other that the walls were a mere arm's length apart. Their shaggy thatched roofs nearly touched. It was only when we'd walked into the clearing at the end of the path that I saw the first glimpse of the water just beyond the rim of the circle of houses. There, the shoreline was flat and unadorned with piers or esplanades. The air was filled with the sound of birds, and the sky was sun-washed blue over a pale blue sea. Fishing boats were tied at the water's edge, where tamarind trees resisted the wind, their trunks split into forks that formed V-shapes, the branches raised both north and south as if the tree were balancing in the crosscurrent of ocean breezes. A young boy in red trunks stood on the limb of one tree, a bicycle tube hanging from his foot as he measured the distance down the beach or back to the road where he casually watched us make our way toward the center of the village. I was reminded of the painting by the African American artist, Hughie Lee-Smith, titled *Boy with a Tire*. The boy in the tree had the same youthful expression, the relief of being left to his own devices to invent a space in the adult world.

Along the beach, fishermen stretched their nets, and women went about their chores. There was none of the formality I'd felt at the Boina settlement; we were simply strangers passing through.

The beach at Aranta was so flat and shallow, I was reminded of the southern coast, near Toliara, where a group of fishermen from a small sea island had waded to shore and offered us lunch from their fresh catch of carp. We had watched them walk back to their pirogues anchored in the shallows about fifty feet from shore. The sandbar was disturbed only when they walked on it. In Aranta, the beach was constantly infused with sand-red silt from the Betsiboka, the waters so vividly stained that

A fishing family returning to their boat, Chanel de Mozambique near Toliara

astronauts reportedly have used it to mark their flight path—an ocean streaked in plumes of red soil like a comet's tail. Even where salt spray darkened the trees, and the tawny yellow sand took hold in the shallows nearest the shore, the hint of red seemed to blur the distinction between the land and the sea, between the houses and the fishing boats. During my time in the village, I felt the lines were equally blurred between friend and stranger. Such was not the case when I met Daniel Stanislas.

The first time I met with Daniel Stanislas, he welcomed me as one poet would welcome another. He was over seventy years old—by Western standards, an old man of retirement age—yet each morning he took his boat into the treacherous waters of the Chanel de Mozambique. The sea had left him with a rugged look, and with his grizzled mustache and

Storyteller, M. Stanislas, Aranta

whiskers, he was handsome at any age. His fingers were long and expressive, despite the paralysis in one hand caused by a blow to the head during the 1947 anticolonial uprising against the French. M. Stanislas was a fisherman and a poet, and like the poets M. Rado and M. Ernest, his keen sense of pride in his cultural history had been honed during that revolution. When I explained my quest for folktales, he said, "These stories we told even when the French were here. But the young people now have lost interest in the stories. It is good to have someone who wants to hear them, even if you come from so far away."

We spent only a brief time with M. Stanislas during that first visit, but the next day we arrived after the evening meal, just before the sun picked up the red glow of laterite in one last burst of color and evening swallowed the horizon. M. Stanislas lit an oil lamp and as he began his stories in the halo of the dim light, the sunset sky turned red as the flesh of blood oranges. I could not have hoped for a more magical setting: the sun reflected off the sand-rinsed palette of the sea, the sound of children laughing as they delayed their chores for one more game before nightfall, young lovers strolling, hand-in-hand, in the thickening light. It was as if I'd entered some enchanted place where I found Jaotombo, the fisherman who fought tricksters, and Ikoto, the doomed child. The doorway to the hut was like an open page of a book, its single window an unblinking eye. Through that opening, I could read the comings and goings of the village while Daniel Stanislas brought me closer to its myths. Outside, the sunlight performed its last rose-red dance of the day, but inside, shadows filled the hut, and even M. Stanislas seemed to be transported to the world of legend as he leaned forward in his chair and let the stories carry us all away.

(Note: M. Stanislas died in his hometown of Aranta in January 1999. The author mourns his passing and doubly values the stories he shared.)

കുകുകുകു

Jadan'Ikoto

Once upon a time, there were two people: a husband and a wife. They had a three-year-old son whose name was Ikoto. The husband was called Jadan'Ikoto (Ikoto's father) and the wife was called Jendrin'Ikoto

(Ikoto's mother). They lived in a small village. One day, Jadan'Ikoto (the father) took his son, Ikoto, walking in the woods to look for honey, as the family was accustomed to doing. As they reached the middle of the woods—though it was very sunny—thunder crashed through the trees and was followed by a thunderstorm. Jadan'Ikoto was worried because his son was still so little and he saw him shivering.

The boy said, "I am so cold, father."

The father answered, "If only you would have agreed to stay with your mother, no misfortune would have happened to you." However, their way home was still so far away.

Then all of a sudden, while they weren't expecting anything, a huge bird, which could lift an ox, flew upon them and took the little boy in its claws. Afterwards, it raised its wings and took Ikoto very high. Jadan'Ikoto tried to catch the bird but he failed. In desperation, he followed them. Up went the bird.

The little boy cried and begged his father, "Father, I am caught and I can't do anything. Take my finger. Hold it tightly. If you run faster, you can catch me."

The father ran, ran, ran with all his strength, somehow growing stronger than usual. But when he got nearer and nearer, the bird flew higher and higher. Finally, the only thing the father could grab was the tip of his son's finger. Still, the bird kept flying higher and higher, and the father was left with nothing but the child's finger. But finally he could see that the bird was growing weary, weary, weary, and ready to leave the boy on a huge rock at the edge of a cave. And truly, the bird did as Jadan'Ikoto expected.

The father called to his son, "My little boy, where are you? What is going on up there?"

"Oh father," the boy cried. "I am lost. Try to climb and take me."

The father managed to climb, climb, climb, and finally he could grab the leg of his son. But when he was near success, a great rock rolled down the cave. He did whatever he could to save his son, but again he failed and was left with nothing more than the child's leg.

The little boy cried and said, "Save me, father. I am dying."

But suddenly, the huge bird returned and filled the cave with mud and stones. So the little boy, buried under mud and stones, was dead. Finally, exhausted and distressed, the father went home. He was desolate. However, on his way back, he kept thinking about what would happen to his wife once she heard the bad news. He hesitated over whether to tell her about the terrible incident or keep quiet. After all, Ikoto was their first and beloved child. So, when he was returned to the village, the father went straight away to the diviner for some advice. He told the diviner what had happened to him and his child. He showed the diviner his child's finger and leg, and told him the child was dead. He asked whether or not he had to speak of this incident to his wife. The diviner told him to find his wife and take her to his hut.

When they were home, his wife asked him, "Where is Ikoto, my child?"

"I lost him," the father answered. "And we have to go together to the diviner since I am sure he is the only one who can find Ikoto. So, let's go there now."

When they were at the diviner's, they said, "We're here, Grandfather," using a name of respect given to diviners.

"Grandfather, our child is lost in the forest," said the father, using the words the diviner had told to him. "So we beg you to find our son and show us where he is now."

The diviner pretended to consult his *sikidy* of grains, beans, and tamarind seeds instead of using the cards diviners have for seeing the future. At last he said to the parents, "Your child is not lost and is not dead."

"But where is he?" asked the parents.

The diviner looked at Jendrin'Ikoto. "A spirit took him and put him in the womb of this woman." Then he asked, "Isn't she your wife?"

"Yes," the father replied.

And the woman, very happy and reassured, asked again. "So, is he here in my womb?"

"Yes, your child is there," the diviner convinced her.

"So when can we see him?" the mother asked.

"Be patient," the diviner said. "Meanwhile we will use these medicines and plants to keep him healthy."

And the woman exclaimed, "I'll see my Ikoto and I will dance at this time."

"You will dance at this time," the diviner said.

After a few months, when the new child was born, the parents were amazed to see how much the child resembled Ikoto. The mother, happy to see her son again, said, "Ikoto my child, what has made you return to my womb?"

But the diviner said nothing. And since his wife was so happy, the husband never told her the sad story of the lost child.

—Daniel Stanislas
(Aranta)

കൈകൈകൈകൈ

Jaotombo, the Fisherman

Once upon a time, there was a man called Jaotombo, which means "grown-up young man." Jaotombo worked as a fisherman. Even though he could catch every kind of fish, he and his wife were still very poor. He was sitting down while fishing because he was hungry and exhausted; then "something" passing by him called out, "Hey, you!"

"Who is that?" Jaotombo answered. He could hear a voice but he could not see anyone.

"You can't see me," the thing said, "so it's I who talk to you. Do you want to be wealthy? Do you want to get some money?"

"Yes, I do want to be wealthy and get some money," said the young man, and his fear vanished at the same time.

"See that wide fairly level ground over there," he was told. "Over there is a huge cave and inside, along the way inside, are meandering paths from the beginning to the end. Nobody has ever entered it. But know that down there is gold, and precious stones, and many kinds of wonderful things. So if you want to be wealthy, go there."

"Where is that place?" the young man asked again.

The voice explained again, and said, "A long time ago there were some people who tried to come into the cave, but they never came back because they were lost in the meandering paths inside the cave. Also, it was said that a long time ago there were people who entered the cave to seek things, but they could never find anything."

Jaotombo said, "So why should I go there?"

"Go over and you'll find something. But this is what I say: when you come to the village, don't change your habits but knit a very long, small rope like a string. When your wife asks about the rope, tell her, "I need this for something." After that, come back here in this place again but don't tell that to anyone else. I'll come here to tell you what you should do next."

The days passed and the man kept knitting the rope. He and his wife had a discussion about the rope, and his wife scolded him for not telling her anything about what he was doing. But he kept silent. When he finished the rope, he went back to the place and called, "Hey, you who can't be seen, you who can't be seen."

"Yes, I am here," the one who can't be seen answered.

"I have come back and these are the ropes," the young man said. He pulled an enormous coil of ropes from a big basket.

Then he was told, "Take that rod in front of the gate, fasten the rod to the rope, then go inside the cave. As you walk, loosen the rope."

Jaotombo went to the cave and did as he was told. He walked along and as he stepped forward, he could see either a very dark thing or a very shiny thing, but he could not see clearly. He could also see many precious objects. He was fascinated and did not know what to do, so the young man said to himself, "This is the very treasure the thing that cannot be seen told me about." Jaotombo took his cloth off as well as his *kitamby*,* and folded them. Then he filled them with the precious objects and was ready to leave the cave. It was dark but the moon was full. He followed the direction of the rope in the meandering cave, and finally reached the gate. He left the coil of the rope in front of the gate and went home.

When he arrived, he told his wife what happened: "My wife, now we're living (meaning: being wealthy)."

"But why?" his wife asked. He spread all of the wonderful objects of precious stones and gold in front of his wife. His wife was so delighted, and she danced. But when the next morning came, she said to her husband, "I'm leaving you."

"Why are you leaving?" her husband asked. "When we were so poor, you didn't leave me but now that we can see the corner, then you leave me?"

"Yes, I'm leaving. I just have enough."

He tried to keep her there, but she didn't stay. It was clear that she'd already made some plans. She left and went right away to her brother's house. "Where are you, my brother? Come by here, we are going to be living," she said. "If my husband could find so many things, because we're brother and sister, we'll go together and get some of those things. That's why I left him."

"Well, you are a true relative, my sister. Let me see those beautiful things." She showed him the precious objects, and when the brother saw them, he was ready to go searching the way his sister's husband did.

Meanwhile, Jaotombo was wondering if his wife might get a bad idea from someone else, or if she might be plotting a bad plan. So he went to the place where the cave was and hid himself behind the gate. In the evening, the woman and her brother actually came by the cave, but Jaotomba remained hidden until they went into the cave. Once they

---

* *Kitamby*: a long piece of material that men used to wear, turning the cloth around their thighs and crossing it between their legs, particularly to hide the sex.

got in and were about to reach the upper level of the cave, Jaotombo cut the rope down, so that they could reach the upper level but they would not be able to come back to the gate. And that is what happened to the brother as the woman waited for him just a few steps away from the gate. The brother couldn't find his way out of the cave, and the people in the village said, "Some people died for nothing because they already knew that this cave belonged to the thing that could not be seen, yet they still went there."

However, the fisherman's wife came back again with one of her other brothers. She tried to use another way to get into the cave. She said to her brother, "Let me wait for you outside the cave while you go up there."

It was dark but the moon was full, as it had been on Jaotombo's visit. The other brother went into the cave. Meanwhile, the woman's former husband still wanted to catch her, so he also went to the cave and hid himself to wait for the one who would pull the rope. But this time, the woman also hid herself to wait for the one who would cut the rope. Finally, they could see each other.

"What're you doing here?" asked the man.

"I came with my brother," the woman replied. "I know you've planned to kill me and my brother."

And they had a big fight. They pushed each other and finally the man fell down into the cave, hit his head, and was covered by the stones and died.

Then, the woman said to her brother, "You see, that is my former husband. He planned to kill us."

And her brother said, "Thank you, my dear sister. If you hadn't been there, I would have been killed." Then they went home and had a happy life. This was the kind of woman who liked her relatives but would betray her husband.

—Daniel Stanislas
(Aranta)

If our departure flight from Mahajanga had not been delayed, I would not have ventured back into the city and put up in a midtown hotel. It was a small hotel, a layover stop for airline personnel, and because of the delayed flight, full of disgruntled passengers who had intended to be on their way elsewhere. We milled around the desk, complaining about the delay, complaining about airlines in general. The desk clerks were rattled, the housekeepers were rattled, the waiters were rattled. After we had checked in, I decided to have a drink on the patio outside the hotel.

It was perfect late-afternoon light, the kind that turned the buildings that same shade of pink as the cliffs at Amborovy Beach. I think I was drinking in the light as much as the glass of wine when I heard the children. At first, I thought it was merely children playing after school, waiting to be called home for supper. But the voices grew louder. A large group, I thought, until I saw them turn the corner. A parade, and not just a small parade. They were marching in formation—fifty, sixty, a hundred children, adult leaders marching beside them every ten yards or so. They went on for three blocks or more, elementary school children hours after school had ended. Not one out of line, not one losing concentration.

"They are practicing for National Day," Tiana said. "Then we have a big parade here, and in Toamasina, Tana, and Toliara. All over Madagascar."

There was something quite beautiful about all of those children, marching with such purpose in preparation for a national holiday. It would be the first bonus I'd receive because my plane had been delayed.

My second bonus came only a few hours later. Because the hotel was so crowded and service had disintegrated to sporadic attendance to the guests, we decided to have dinner elsewhere. On the way back to the hotel from the restaurant, we walked past a line of shops that were closed for the evening, but in one a window display of geodes caught my eye. I had been aware of the beautiful rock formations in the Mahajanga area, but until my departure was delayed, I hadn't found the time to search for any shops that specialized in geodes and polished rocks. I would have missed the shop if it had not been for the blue light from the cutter's torch reflected in the rock facades. I tapped on the window and he let us in.

For almost an hour, we examined shelves of geodes, fossils, and shells. The geodes had been split to reveal the bed of crystals nested inside their stone pouches: rose quartz, agate, jasper, citrine, and chalcedony. Some caught the patterns of earth; others were fossilized stones that echoed the sea. One, filled with striated patterns of rose crystal, looked like a slice of the cliffs over Amborovy Beach. The geode next to it held a bouquet of amethyst, the color varied from lilac to deep purple. In another, sea-green quartz was caught in the pocket like miniature stalagmites. The larger pieces were spectacular, like small caves with jeweled walls. And the fossils were no less spectacular—evidence of evolutionary shifts trapped in layers of rock, fingerprints of a world that no longer existed. I bought a pyramid of polished obsidian and an egg-shaped section of stripped agate, the sides so smooth, the surfaces could have been mirrors.

Ny feno tsy miko bana.
The full sail does not tremble.

CHAPTER IX

ONLY THE SEA BEYOND

The vessels that sail from the coast of Malabar for this island
perform the voyage in twenty or twenty-five days, but in their
returning voyage are obliged to struggle for three months; so
strong is the current of water, which constantly runs southward.
—*Travels of Marco Polo [The Venetian]*
("The Great Island of Madagascar")

If you journey south from India, or east from Africa, or around the world from any place on the globe, you might reach Nosy Bé. At least, this is what sailors whisper on nights when the wind is calm and the Indian Ocean seems to stretch into forever. But take care. When you finally sail free of the ocean's grasp, you might miss the first glimpse of a string of sequin-green islands, flung like beads away from the red soil of the western shores of Madagascar into the Chanel de Mozambique. The African coast is a scant two hundred miles away, but from these islands nothing seems close, not when the next continent is Antarctica and the ocean is bigger than the rest of the world. But some have made it this far—and some, the sailors say, no farther. So you let the surf roll you in. Once beached, you smell the hint of mountains as the wind tumbles down from the Ambre, and with it, smoke from a villager's cooking fire. Take a deeper breath. In the hazy light of seductive evenings, the sweet scents of ylang-ylang, figs, and mangoes dance inside the moss-thick odors of a mud-choked river or a glassy lake. At night, the old-man-of-the-trees wraps his long tail around a branch and stares at you, his eyes bright as marbles and full of those ageless questions lemurs have always had about men. But day or night, insects, as ancient as the lemurs, click-clack wing against shell, gill against leg in a rattle of sounds that once might have echoed the warnings of a pirate's saber, a slave trader's riata, or a fisherman's gutting knife. The setting is idyllic: blue sky and ocean, islands as enticing as sirens, the sun swimming at the rim of the horizon.

Under the bright sun, the sea sparkles with pearl-drops of light. Sunsets are cloaked in every shade from orange and pink to magenta, violet, and bawdy red—magnificantly stretching out behind islands of low mountains draped in purple and lilac mist.

On the leeward side of Nosy Bé, in what was once an Indian settlement, there is an old soap factory. Masked by flame trees, the foot-thick sand and coral walls form an escarpment that faces the sea. The factory is more fortress than industry, a structure built to withstand the siege of both weather and intruders. The wall protects the factory and the hillside behind it on which an abundance of soap plants still flourish among the breadfruit and mango trees. There are flowers everywhere: ylang-ylang, geranium, and vetiver holding their own in a gathering of bright red pepper plants. The lushness of the hillside softens the graying ruins of the soap factory, its vast wooden vats waxed with the remnants of *savony*. Inside the mixing sheds, dusty work benches stand ready as if their owners will return tomorrow, but the stale odors of abandonment prevail. Outside the building, you breathe in the fragrance of flowers and turn toward the sea. From any point along the wall, you can watch fishing pirogues making their way into the channel, their lateen-rigged sails more Arab than Indian. This is the place where slave traders and pirates from India and Africa have stopped to rest. And it is here that the sultan of Zanzibar and the French governor of the Bourbon Islands offered the Sakalava protection from the Malagasy monarchy. The animosity lingers still. "You are going back to Madagascar," some say when you leave Nosy Bé. But for those who stayed, those who abandoned the dream of conqueror and learned how to live with the Sakalava—the Arabs and Indians, the Russians and Chinese—this island has been their haven. The graveyards in Hell-Ville, and on Nosy Raty, the "island of the dead," offer evidence of their sojourns. Still, the islands remain seemingly unscathed, jade green centers with ribbons of white sand and palm trees bordering the blue blue ocean.

From island to island—Nosy Bé, Nosy Komba, Nosy Tanikely, and Nosy Sakatia—sweet ylang-ylang vied with the scents of orchids and banana blossoms, and the chittering of birds pierced the air. On Nosy Tanikely, where electric blue kingfishers skimmed the waves for food, flying foxes flittered in the treetops like large butterflies, their squeaks more like bats than foxes. I saw them in a brief spread of webbed arms and legs, then they were gone, folding into the limbs of palms until tree and fox were one.

On Nosy Komba, it was the plaintive calls of lemurs that added to the cacophony of sounds. The lemurs of Nosy Komba were doll faced and soft as kittens. Over the years, they had been touristed and had come to expect visitors. When we stepped off the boat from Nosy Bé, the villagers only half acknowledged our landing. (On our way back to the wharf, they would track us down to buy beautifully embroidered tablecloths and linen in lace patterns of zebu, lemur, and flower motifs.) But as soon as we entered the Reserve area, the lemurs were on the alert. With the flash of one banana, they came running. When I insisted on holding onto the banana I offered, one of them simply ate it while sitting on my head. It was the only time I can remember my head being used as a dining room table.

Nosy Komba was not my first encounter with lemurs. A month earlier, in the southern part of Madagascar at Fort Dauphin, Tiana and I had taken an excursion to the Berenty Reserve.

To reach Berenty, we'd traveled through the spiny forest, the home of the Antandroy, "people of the thorns." The landscape was somewhat forbidding, the parched earth broken by an occasional hut, a scattering of bottle trees, thickets of giant cacti that reached their thorny arms skyward, and sisal plantations big as Texas ranches—all of it separated by

Stelae marking Antanosy tombs near Taolañaro

oases of freshwater streams draped in heavy foliage. But for all of this, the land seemed empty, the temperature soaring under a sun that hung in the cloudless sky like a bare light bulb. Even a cluster of stelae marking Antanosy tombs seemed untended and lonely in that treeless stretch of sun-parched grass. Nothing moved except the lizards and sand flies. But in the emerald green stretches of water and trees, shadows teemed with life.

Once, when we crossed a one-lane bridge, I saw a malachite-colored spider, the size of a dinner plate, suspended from the girders by its long long legs. In Tana, in the old courtyard of the Queen's Palace, a colony of obsidian black spiders knit together an arbor of trees high in the hills above the city.* They hung in the cat's cradle of webs, seemingly in mid-air, like strange seedpods or thousands of jet beads flung from a ball gown

---

* The palace was destroyed in a fire in 1996.

and caught in a gossamer lacework of light. "Guardian of the bridge," I told Tiana as we crept past the bridge-tending spider. "Must be looking for trolls," I added.

"The spiders look for insects," Tiana said. "Do you hear them? They are making noises, like hissing cockroaches. You remember the cockroaches?" she laughed.

I listened to the clatter of insects dislodged by the weight of the bus, a kind of ground swell like the white noise of machines on the blink, and I shuddered, remembering the cockroaches of Toliara.

"They're calling you," she'd laughed. "They're saying: Colleen, where are you?"

I growled and wished the spiders a full meal every night. I still had the image of those spiders in my head when we'd reached Berenty. I think I half expected the lemurs of Berenty to be as unpleasant as their insect neighbors. What I found were shy creatures that were sometimes cautious, sometimes almost playful. I caught glimpses of them as I walked through the heavily forested reserve. Once, I turned a corner and discovered several snow-white *sifaka* dancing in a meadow on their hind legs like disco patrons or ancient sun worshipers (take your pick, but it looked like a get-down boogie to me). Unlike the smaller lemurs, the *sifaka* seemed tall, long limbed, their white fur glistening in the sun. They changed positions, balanced, and made small jetés, the black masks of their faces directed toward the sun. But as soon as I pulled my camera from its pouch, they stopped, leapt into the trees, and eyed me suspiciously. I kept my camera ready from that point on. Later, I heard a rustling noise behind me, or at least I thought I had. I had passed under some trees where the lemurs were singing, their vocalizations more like the mewings of babies than the calls of animals. More often than not, I'd heard them but could not see them, so the sound hadn't surprised me. But that time, when I turned, several ring-tailed lemurs were on the road behind me. They stopped when I stopped; moved when I moved—fast or slow, sideways or not, their splayed tails like black and white exclamation points quivering with the mischief of it all. They were mimicking

With Tiana on a road in the spiny forest, near Berenty

me, but that was as close as they'd let me get. At least, that group had allowed me several photos. Only by accident did I catch a picture of a sweet faced brown lemur at treetop height. I'd simply kept clicking the shutter in the direction of the sound and caught him, peering down at me, the intruder in his forest. Then he'd folded back into the trees.

On Nosy Bé, I quickly understood why Marco Polo had dubbed the outer isles of Madagascar "the perfumed islands." Breezes were spiced with the scent of flowers mixed with the salty spray of the sea. It was a scent I had not smelled so clearly anywhere else in Madagascar, perhaps because on the sea islands there was less traffic and, aside from the ylang-ylang perfume factory, virtually no pollution from industry. Under the fragrance of ylang-ylang, jasmine, and frangipani, I caught a trace of something that reminded me of the maili plants in Hawaii. The air was redolent with that smell, and the weather was Hawaiian balmy. Like Hawaii, the island had the usual collections of shops carrying swim wear and fossils from the sea, but Hell-Ville, the largest town on Nosy Bé (named after Admiral de Hell, the nineteenth-century governor of Ile de Réunion), had a small-town aura about it. Everyone seemed happier than in Tana, tolerating, of course, the tourists. Even the lambas, worn more in Pacific Island style than Indonesian, seemed more colorful. But what amazed me each morning was the stretch of sandy beach with clear waters and calm winds. At the water's edge, I almost didn't need a snorkel mask to see the schools of fish in the currents close to the shore. Palm trees, ruffled by the wind, sounded like the swishing of hula dancers' skirts. The cry of shorebirds prancing at the edge of the surf blended perfectly with the feeling of island life, the scent of ylang-ylang soothing the warming wind that stirred the leaves.

The Catholic Mission in Andoany (Hell-Ville) was on a quiet little cul-de-sac not far from the center of town. Its architecture was similar to that of other abbeys I'd seen in Madagascar: stone and timber construction of medieval French design, so simple and stark the buildings seemed to belong more to a castle keep than a church. The parish, rectory, school, and infirmary enclosed a courtyard of gray cobblestones, the sameness of color relieved by the profusion of flowers growing along the garden wall. We had gone there to find Father Robert Jaovelo-Dzao. I had heard of his work on Malagasy folktales and the oral tradition, most of which had been published in France. I had expected to talk with him only briefly, but although it was the middle of the day and he was still busy with classes, he made some time for us. We met with him in the rectory, in an office paneled with books, a rare sight in a country where books were

Storyteller, Father Jaovelo-Dzao, Nosy Bé

often scarce even at the universities. But Father Dzao had studied at the
Sorbonne, and his library reflected the work he'd done there.

At first, I took him to be serious, this scholar-priest, but as soon as he
smiled, I was put at ease. I couldn't help it. I told him he reminded me of
Sidney Poitier, especially his smile. Tiana agreed. Father Dzao laughed.
"But M. Poitier is a man of many talents. I am but a priest."

"M. Poitier does not know the stories of Madagascar," I said.

Again, he smiled. He told me that he was interested in what similari-
ties I'd found in the stories that I'd thus far collected, and was worried
that perhaps he would have nothing to add. I assured him that my interests had more to do with traditional stories of recurring themes than an
analysis of the stories. He talked about his study of the different types of
folktales, especially those used in the schools and those translated into
French. When I asked if he remembered any stories he'd heard as a child,

he nodded. "But he has no time for those stories today," Tiana said. I sighed. I'm sure the sigh was prompted by my memory of the Boina settlement in Mahajanga.

"He will meet with us tomorrow," Tiana said.

"Before the evening services," Father Dzao added in French. We had only a few more minutes to chat before he rushed away, summoned back to his duties somewhere else in the abbey.

There was no reason for my anxiety. Father Dzao met with us the next day, and although rushed, as usual, began to talk about the stories he remembered from his childhood. He would tell us one, he said, that he had not yet translated into French. And then he began, in the true style of a storyteller, by saying: "Perhaps I will not remember the entire story, and perhaps I will. We heard this many times when I was a child."

There is always a sense of magic when the storyteller begins, a feeling that time has stopped, if for only that moment. I knew it was early evening—the light filtered through the beveled glass windows was growing dim. In that room with its fireplace and walls of books on theology and folklore, Father Dzao's voice allowed us to glimpse, for a moment, the spell that every child has known under the gaze of the storyteller. And Tiana, holding the tape recorder, nodded her head as if she were greeting old friends.

◈◈◈◈◈

Betombokoantsoro: Faralahy Bikesa, the Monster

Once upon a time, there were three sisters. All of them were of the marriageable age and they were just waiting to be asked. Their parents tried to prepare them for marriage, and didn't cease to give them advice and lessons. They used to say, "Before getting married, you don't have to throw yourselves on the first man who approaches. Choose your future husband well." But the daughters laughed and waited for their husbands.

One day, the monster, Rakakabe, came to their village. He went to their house in order to meet their parents. When he knocked on the door, their parents called, "Come in. Why do you come to our house?"

"I'd like to ask for your daughter's hand," he said. But since he appeared as a beautiful young man, he didn't say he was a monster. Instead, he told them that his favorite wife would be the youngest girl. As was the custom, if the youngest married before the others, the older sisters had to follow her.

"Well," the parents answered, "before our daughters go with their husband, they have to consult their grandmother to get her blessing."

The girls went to see their grandmother and said, "Grandma, we are going to get married."

"You are going to get married? All of you?"

"Yes, we are."

"So, here are some *tognotogno*," she said, and gave them some small round baskets, plaited with straw and nested one inside the other. "And here are some rice and some eggs. Take them with you just to protect you." Then she blessed them and said, "May what you do go well. May you be well. That is what I ask God and the ancestors."

According to the custom, the husband could not live in the place where he asked for his wife's hand, and he could not live in his wife's land. He had to take his new wife to his village.

The girls had a young brother whose body was covered by scabies and they didn't like him. Before they left, this brother asked to come with them, but they refused.

"You may not go with us," they said.

"I want to go with you, elder sisters," the brother said.

"Never," they said.

"Take me with you. I beg you," he cried.

"No, you can't go there," they told him. But finally, they felt pity for the child, and they agreed to take him when they left the village. So they left with their husband. They walked, walked, walked to reach the village where the monster lived. When they saw the monster's house, they were fascinated with its beautiful roof and its beautiful furniture.

They were amazed and talked to each other: "Oh! it's wonderful, amazing. We'll be comfortable and won't want to go back home."

"Oh yes," they all cried, and thought of how they would enjoy their lives there with the monster.

As for the monster, he went to work in the fields all day and came back only when night fell. That was what he always did. However, the youngest brother thought there was something wrong with his behavior since each time he returned home, he had his long tail hanging out. But the sisters could only see the beautiful house and beautiful furniture. The boy watched the monster and was very surprised and terrified when he returned at night and began singing:

"Are you sleeping, are you sleeping, eldest sister? Are you sleeping?" The eldest sister didn't answer because she really was sleeping. The monster was delighted and said to himself:

"Ah! everybody is sleeping." And he asked again. "Are you sleeping, are you sleeping, middle sister? Are you sleeping?" But the middle sister was sleeping soundly and did not answer. The monster was happy and said again:

"Ah! everybody is sleeping." So once more, he asked, "Are you sleeping, are you sleeping, youngest sister?" And because the youngest sister was also sleeping, she did not say anything. The monster was delighted, and dancing, he said again:

"Ah! everybody is sleeping." And he asked for the last time, "Are you sleeping, are you sleeping, little brother with scabies. Are you sleeping?"

"No, I'm not sleeping. I'm not sleeping, my brother-in-law, I'm not sleeping."

"Oh, what's happening to you, my brother-in-law?" asked the monster.

"Well, there are many mosquitoes in the room and I can't manage to kill them. What do I do?"

So the monster killed all of the mosquitoes by eating them until he was full. And the brother with scabies said, "Oh! I'm going to sleep soundly now because there is not one mosquito left."

When morning came, the monster did as he always did and when night fell, he came back again and it was the same question. But the young boy always found an excuse to trick the monster. One day, he told his sisters, "Well, my sisters, don't you realize that your husband is a monster?"

His sisters told him, "You're so stupid. That's why we refused to take you here. We told you to stay at home and now you invent this story that our husband is a monster. Be careful, or we will hit you."

But the boy told them again, "Since you always sleep so soundly at night, you've never known that he was about to eat you. But let's see what he will do."

Finally they made a plan to see what really happened during the night. That day, the monster did as usual and that night, he came home singing the same questions. However, the sisters and their brother were waiting for him to come home and they just pretended to be sleeping. The monster entered, dragging his dazzling long tail:

"Are you sleeping, are you sleeping, eldest sister? Are you sleeping?" The eldest did not answer. The monster was delighted and said: "Ah! everybody is sleeping."

And he asked again, "Are you sleeping, are you sleeping, middle sister? Are you sleeping?" She too did not say anything. The monster was very happy and said again, "Ah! everybody is sleeping," and he danced with his dazzling tail.

He asked again, "Are you sleeping, are you sleeping, youngest sister? Are you sleeping?" But she didn't answer. The monster was dancing and said, "Everybody is sleeping." Finally he asked, "Are you sleeping, are you sleeping, brother with scabies? Are you sleeping?"

But the boy wanted to frighten his sisters and he told them he wasn't going to answer. They were terrified and begged him to answer. "Do answer, please, our dear brother. We are going to die if you don't say anything."

And so he said, "I am not sleeping, my brother-in-law. I'm not sleeping."

"What's still happening to you, my dear brother-in-law?" asked the monster.

"There are too many fleas in this room. I try to sleep and they jump on me. I swat one. Then I try to sleep again and another one jumps on me and I can't sleep."

So the monster killed all of the fleas by eating them, every one.

Seeing this, the sisters were surprised and frightened. But finally, they believed their brother.

Early the next morning, the monster went out as usual to the field. Once he disappeared, the sisters left the house with their brother who had scabies and ran away. They ran, ran, ran. In running, they threw back the rice their grandmother had blessed and continued on their way. When night fell, the monster returned home and was ready to do as he always did.

"Are you sleeping, are you sleeping, eldest sister? Are you sleeping?" No answer.

"Are you sleeping, are you sleeping, middle sister? Are you sleeping?" No answer.

"Are you sleeping, are you sleeping, youngest sister? Are you sleeping?" No answer.

"Are you sleeping, are you sleeping, brother with scabies? Are you sleeping?" No answer.

Now the monster was happy and ready to feast. He was ready to eat them even if he had begun to suspect something. But when he saw nobody was there, he was so furious, he ran like lightning to pursue them. He ran for a while and saw some rice spread on the ground.

"Here's my rice," he said, and picked up the kernels and took them back to his village.

Meanwhile the three sisters and their brother threw away the eggs, which turned into a very large river. The monster returned to pursue them again and when he reached the river, he had to build a wooden canoe since he could not swim in a river so deep and wide, and crossing it would take him a very long time.

By this time, the three sisters and their brother had safely reached their village. When they told the villagers what had happened, their parents immediately hid them. Soon, the monster came, running like the wind. But the villagers were ready for him. They brought knives and swords, and when he entered the village, they tied him with a rope and stabbed him until he died.

From that time, the daughters truly learned a moral lesson from their parents. Before getting engaged, try to look out. Don't throw yourself at the first one who approaches. You have to choose well who is going to be your husband.

—as told by Father Jaovelo-Dzao
(Nosy Bé)

By the time I reached Nosy Bé, at the end of my journey through Madagascar, much of what I saw seemed as familiar as places I had called home. Instead of months, I felt as if my visit had taken years, as if each road, while bringing me to some place new, would circle around and let me once again see its beginnings. How different it had all seemed when I arrived, in those first few days in Tana when I'd almost needed a map to help me make my way from La Karthala to the Zoma market. In a few months, I'd learned how to clock the distances between villages, and look at the amazing landscape with a keener sense of those subtle differences in colors and shapes, however brilliant.

One night at Nosy Bé, as I looked up at the sky that was full of stars in constellations I couldn't name, I remembered my visit to Ambalavao, a village in the Highlands. I had been in the country for only a few weeks at that time, and I saw everything with untrained eyes. That wasn't difficult with the night sky. The stars in the Southern Hemisphere were like sequins sprinkled across a desert of black sand, so close I believed I could almost touch them. That night in Ambalavao, when Tiana, Haingo, and I had been walking back to the hotel after a late supper, I'd looked at the sky and marveled at the multitude of stars. "I hope I will find many stories here," I'd said, not so much to spur anyone into action, but simply to say something while I was staring into the eyes of the universe. I had no sooner spoken than a shooting star streaked across the heavens. It was my opportunity, I thought, to share some folklore I'd heard as a child. "My grandmother told me that any time you see a shooting star and make a wish, it will come true," I'd said.

"Yes, it is prophecy," Tiana had said.

"I think you will have your stories," Haingo assured me.

He was right, although I cannot say if it was my wishing that made it so. What I do know is that for a while I entered the world of storytellers and poets, a world where metaphor reigned and ancestors held wisdom. *Avy tsy nangeha nasesiky ny raza*, a Malagasy proverb declares— "The ancestors come into our lives like guests who need no invitation." And as I think about the stories and poems I've gathered, I want to paraphrase that quote to read: These tales are like the ancestors. They need no invitation.

INDEX

Page numbers in boldface type indicate illustrations.